Beyond Violence

BEYOND VIOLENCE

Religious Sources of Social Transformation
in Judaism, Christianity, and Islam

Edited by JAMES L. HEFT, S.M.

FORDHAM UNIVERSITY PRESS
New York • 2004

The Abrahamic Dialogues Series, No. 1
ISSN 1548-4130

Library of Congress Cataloging-in-Publication Data

Beyond violence : religious sources of social transformation in Judaism, Christianity, and Islam / edited by James L. Heft.—1st. ed.
    p. cm.—(The Abrahamic dialogues series ; no. 1)
  Includes bibliographical references and index.
  ISBN 0-8232-2333-7 (hardcover)—ISBN 0-8232-2334-5 (pbk.)
    1. Peace—Religious aspects—Congresses. 2.Violence—Religious aspects—Congresses. I. Heft, James. II. Series.
BL65.P4B49 2004
201.'76—dc22

                                                              2004001737

Printed in the United States of America
08 07 06 05 04   5 4 3 2 1
First edition

DEDICATION

This volume contains the major papers given at an international conference titled "Beyond Violence: Religious Sources for Social Transformation." Held at the University of Southern California on May 5–7, 2003, the conference drew more than two hundred participants. Jews, Christians, and Muslims honestly and thoughtfully considered how their religious traditions could become greater forces for justice and peace. I dedicate this volume to those individuals who collaborated with me in every phase of planning: Mr. Dafer Dakhil of the Omar Ibn Al-Khattab Foundation, Dr. Reuven Firestone of Hebrew Union College-Jewish Institute of Religion, Dr. Donald E. Miller of the Center for Religion and Civic Culture at the University of Southern California, and Ms. Brie Loskota, the conference director who generously assisted in editing this volume. I dedicate this volume also to those who provided important support for the entire effort: Dr. Steven B. Sample, President of the University of Southern California; Dr. Joseph Aoun, Dean of the College of Letters, Arts and Sciences, USC; Dr. Lewis M. Barth, Dean of HUC-JIR, Los Angeles; and Mr. Edward P. Roski Jr., friend and supporter of the Institute for Advanced Catholic Studies.

Fr. James L. Heft, S.M.
November 16, 2003

CONTENTS

PREFACE: BEYOND VIOLENCE THROUGH DIALOGUE AND COOPERATION

Leonard Swidler

Religion today is at the heart of violence around the world: in Northern Ireland, Sri Lanka, Kashmir, the Middle East, Bosnia, Kosovo, Azerbaijan/Armenia, Cyprus, Iraq, Sudan, and elsewhere. Religion should instead be at the heart of the solution.

How is it that religion, one of the most sublime activities of humanity, has so often through the centuries—even until today—been a motivation for the most heinous of human activities? It is because of the very nature of religion that it can be both: *Corruptio optimae pessima,* "the corruption of the best becomes the worst."

Religion is "an explanation of the *ultimate* meaning of life, and how to live accordingly, based on some notion of the Transcendent, with the four C's: Creed, Code of Ethics, Cult of Worship, Community-Structure." Religion does not attempt to explain just part of life, as do, for example, such disciplines as physics (the physical dimension), chemistry (the chemical dimension), biology (the living dimension), psychology (the inner human dimension), and sociology (the interhuman dimension). Rather, religion attempts to provide a comprehensive explanation of the entirety of life. Consequently, religion tends to be *absolute.*

"Absolute" stems from the Latin *ab* (from) *solvere* (to solve, finish, limit), meaning literally *un-limited.* Hence, religions tend to make unlimited truth claims (my way or the highway). However, during the last two hundred years, we humans have become increasingly aware that all truth claims—that is, all statements about reality—are necessarily limited. This is true even on the most basic level, such as when I truthfully state, "The door is closed" (and it really is). Even though the statement accurately describes the door in relation to its frame, it is still a true statement only within certain limits, for I can also say many other true things about the door. I can speak about its color, weight, and size.

"So what?" one might ask. If it is true that every statement about reality is necessarily limited, not un-limited (ab-solute) even when describing simple physical things, how much more likely is it that our statements about reality are not absolute when speaking of the most complex of realities, "the *ultimate* meaning of life," religion.

Consequently, we come to realize that our religion—all religions!—even when we are convinced that it tells us the truth, cannot be un-limited, ab-solute, in its description of the ultimate meaning of life. There are aspects of the meaning of life that others with different experiences, asking different questions, and using different concepts, cultures, and languages will be able to tell us that we would not otherwise know because we do not have or use their experiences, questions, concepts, cultures, and languages. Hence, if we wish to grasp ever more truth (for, as Jesus said, "The truth will make you free"), we need to be in dialogue with those of different religions to learn from them, and they from us. Then our understanding of the "ultimate meaning of life" will expand and deepen, and hence also will our ability to "live accordingly."

Thus, in the third millennium, religion needs to become less and less part of the problem and increasingly more of the solution through dialogue and cooperation. To this end the Institute for Advanced Catholic Studies at the University of Southern California has here joined with Jewish, Muslim, and secular institutions to foster that dialogue and cooperation, first among the Abrahamic religions and modernity, as well as all the religions and ideologies of the world.

Beyond Violence

INTRODUCTION: RELIGIOUS SOURCES FOR SOCIAL TRANSFORMATION IN JUDAISM, CHRISTIANITY, AND ISLAM

James L. Heft

Especially since the religious wars of the sixteenth and seventeenth centuries, many people in Europe have linked religion with violence. Bloody conflicts between Catholics and Protestants, and then between Protestants and other Protestants, lasted for decades. Once the leaders of the Enlightenment added to the horrors of these religious wars the memories of the Crusades, and especially the Inquisition, they concluded that if religion were excluded as a force from public life, violence could be minimized. They believed that once "privatized," religion would no longer be a source of violence. The public sphere would then be governed, they assumed, by people who followed the light of their own reason. After all, they thought, everyone has the ability to reason, even people who have no faith. In fact, some Enlightenment thinkers claimed that people without any religious faith would be more reasonable than those whose passions were fueled and judgments shaped by religion.

But by the end of the twentieth century, most observers of the international scene came to realize that religion resists privatization. Moreover, it became obvious, to at least some, that religion profoundly affects world events. When in 1979 the public demanded to know how the CIA had failed to anticipate the revolution in Iran, Admiral Stansfield Turner explained that although the agency had carefully tracked Iranian markets, cinema, demographics and publishing, "the only thing we paid no attention to was religion, because it has no power in the modern world."[1] Some observers, particularly neoconservatives in the United States, believe that since the Persian Gulf war in 1991, the terrorist attacks on the World Trade Towers and the Pentagon on September 11, 2001, and subsequent wars in Afghanistan and Iraq, we cannot avoid a "clash of civilizations,"[2] and more specifically, a clash between the West and Islam.

More clear-sighted than Turner and the CIA, and more hopeful than those who foresee an inevitable violent confrontation between civilizations, is theologian Hans Küng, whose commitment to and long-standing involvement with interreligious dialogue led him to the now oft-repeated conviction: No peace among nations without peace among the religions. No peace among the religions without dialogue between the religions. No dialogue between the religions without global ethical criteria. No survival of our globe without a global ethic.

Admittedly, the construction of "global ethical criteria" boggles the mind. A dialogue between religions, however, is imaginable; in fact, it is already taking place. A recent fruitful example of a dialogue among three religious traditions, Judaism, Christianity and Islam, took place at the University of Southern California in May 2003. The chapters of this book contain the major addresses presented at that international conference, titled "Beyond Violence: Religious Sources for Social Transformation." From all over the world, this conference brought together devout Muslims, Jews, and Christians, who, precisely because they are devout, feel compelled to work for reconciliation, peace, and justice. In other words, this conference made more visible an important role that religion can, does, and ought to play in public affairs: being a vehicle for peaceful social transformation. Dozens of international conferences have of late explored the relationship of religion to violence; few, however, have explored how religion contributes to the work of peace and reconciliation. None, to our knowledge, has brought together Jews, Christians, and Muslims, both academics and community activists, to explore how their religious commitments have helped them be ministers of peace and reconciliation.

Serious interreligious dialogue is, historically speaking, only in its infancy. The purpose of interreligious dialogue is not always clear. Is it conversion? Better mutual understanding? Collaboration without any effort at conversion? Is the point for a Christian, for example, to help a Muslim become a better Muslim or a Jew a better Jew? Is it presumptuous to even think that the profound and intimate things of God can be the object of a dialogue, however respectfully conducted? Answers to these questions vary and at times contradict each other. Two things are certain: people of different religions mix with each other more than ever before, and respect for people of other religions is better than violence.

Not everyone thinks dialogue is a good thing. Some oppose it because they see no gain; in other words, they believe they already possess all the truth needed. Some oppose dialogue with a particular religion. Even before the September 11 terrorist attacks, prominent members of the religious right in the United States attacked Islam and the Qur'an. Since then, many of the same prominent conservative religious individuals in the United States have opposed dialogue with Islam. According to Franklin Graham, the son of Billy Graham and now director of his father's vast evangelical enterprise, Islam is "a very evil and wicked religion." Evangelist-broadcaster Pat Robertson described Muhammad as "an absolute wild-eyed fanatic." Taking the caricature even further, Reverend Jerry Vines, past president of the Southern Baptist convention, described Muhammad as a "demon-possessed pedophile."[3] In fairness to most evangelical Protestants in the United States, it should be noted that at the very same time that the "Beyond Violence" conference was taking place at the University of Southern California in Los Angeles, the National Association of Evangelicals and the Institute on Religion and Democracy cosponsored a forum in Washington, D.C., at which prominent evangelicals strongly criticized the negative generalizations of other more conservative evangelicals about Islam, but still supported their right to proselytize to Muslims.

Islam is not the only religion people distort and misunderstand. An equally distorted picture of modern Judaism results when anyone identifies Judaism with the policies of the Israeli government. Within Israel itself, deeply diverse understandings of Judaism challenge each other as to how the state should conduct itself with regard to the Palestinians. Even wider divisions of opinion concerning the policies of Israel can be found among American Jews. In the United States, since the end of the Second Vatican Council in 1965, the Jewish-Christian dialogue has borne much fruit. Rabbis Irving Greenberg and Reuven Firestone enriched the conference as orthodox and reform Jews, respectively.

The great diversity among Jews, Christians, and Muslims created an opportunity for the organizers of the "Beyond Violence" conference. How can the rich diversity of these religions be best represented? After some discussion, we identified two criteria for inviting speakers. First, we wanted individuals who would be able to address in ways we thought insightful the theme of the conference: the contributions religious traditions can and do make to positive social transformation. Second, we wanted to invite well-qualified scholars, so that even if they did not personally represent all the branches of their own religious tradition, they would be informed and fair in what they had to say. We were fortunate in that nearly all of our first choices for main speakers accepted our invitations. Only one, the late Alija Ali Izetbegovic, the former president of Bosnia, had to decline because of ill health. But in his place, we were fortunate to have His Eminence the Grand Mufti of Bosnia-Herzegovina, Dr. Mustafa Ceric. The Muslim planners of the conference did an extraordinary job of including a wide range of speakers from their tradition.

The primary purpose of the conference was neither to proselytize nor to collaborate, though many of the participants came to a deeper knowledge of and respect for religious traditions other than their own. Rather, the conference was designed to explore how these three great religious traditions provide the resources needed for the work of justice and reconciliation. Besides scholars, we also invited individuals who, sometimes at the risk of their own lives, make use of those religious resources in their work. We avoided any denial or cover-up of religion's well-known complicity in violence. For centuries believers have in many instances mistakenly thought that their religion called them to commit acts of violence. Governments and extremist groups often co-opt religion for their own violent purposes. Rather, effort was made to look honestly at the historical and textual records, admit that at times all three religious traditions have fueled acts of violence, and then focus directly on the potential of each tradition to be religious sources of peaceful social transformation.

SCHOLARS AND ACTIVISTS

The conference brought together both scholars and religious activists. All the religious activists, nine in number, were asked to describe in several concurrent breakout sessions their work and how their religious tradition motivated them in that work. These people included a Palestinian Muslim psychiatrist, Samah Jabr, who spoke of the effects of the ongoing conflict in Israel; an American rabbi, Arik Ascherman, who lives in Israel and works for human rights among Jews, Christians, and Muslims; an Anglican priest, Michael Lapsley, who had both hands blown off and an eye destroyed by a 1990 letter bomb sent him by the South African government, but who has continued to devote his life to healing victims of violence; a Catholic sister, Filo Shizue Hirota, who works with Japanese "comfort women," victims of government-sponsored sexual abuse during World War II; a Catholic priest, Michael Kennedy, who works to end violence among gangs of youth in East Los Angeles; a Muslim man, Yasser Aman, who operates a free clinic in south central Los Angeles for indigents of all faiths and no faith; a Jewish social worker, Melodye Feldman, who directs a nonprofit grassroots organization that specializes in helping youth from different religions become peacemakers; another Jewish woman, Stephanie Fingeroth, who organizes Jewish groups to work at issues of women's health, sustainable agriculture, and income generation in developing nations; and finally a Muslim accountant, Naim Shah, who directs the faith-based nonprofit ILM Foundation that provides food for the hungry and helps the unemployed develop marketable skills.

Each of these nine dedicated believers and activists explained their work and how their religious tradition moved them to do that work. Their explanations and testimonies added an intensity and realism to the conference that academic exchanges typically lack. Moreover, the frequent exchanges between activists and the scholars helped keep the academics more grounded in reality and the activists more reflective about their work. Their lively and sometimes tense exchanges have been transcribed, and parts of them will appear in a separate publication edited by Professor Donald E. Miller of the University of Southern California's Center for Religion and Civic Culture.

THE SIX SCHOLARLY ADDRESSES

Six academics, two from each of the three religious traditions, explored the conference theme in ways that drew on their special competencies. First, we asked three of the speakers, Rabbi Irving Greenberg, Professor Charles Taylor, and Dr. Mustafa Ceric, to address the general theme of the conference. Greenberg is an Orthodox Jew with a Harvard doctorate and a deep commitment to the renewal of Judaism in contemporary but faithful forms. Professor Taylor is an internationally recognized philosopher who at one time was personally involved in Canadian politics and brings to his analysis of violence not only a philosophical perspective, but also a grasp of the social sciences and history. Mustafa Ceric has a doctorate from the University of Chicago and has lived through the violence suffered by the people of Bosnia; he embodies a vision of Islam that manifests a familiarity with both the West and the East.

We asked our other three major speakers, Reuven Firestone, Scott Appleby, and Mohamed Fathi Osman, each an accomplished scholar in his own religious tradition, to highlight the resources within their respective traditions for the work of justice and reconciliation. We also asked them to explain whether their traditions have supported violence in any way. And finally, we asked them to reflect on how well in their judgment believers from their own tradition have found within it a resource for the works of justice and reconciliation.

It is significant that the six speakers did not overlap in terms of the content of their presentations. In fact, despite the single focus of the conference, none of them approached the theme in exactly the same way. Each of them shed a sufficiently different light on the conference theme that both problems and possibilities for faith-based social transformation become clearer.

Rabbi Greenberg's presentation, "Religion as a Force for Reconciliation and Peace: A Jewish Analysis," made clear at the outset that violence in the name of religion should be called *chillul hashem*—

the desecration of God's name. It is the responsibility of each religion to correct itself, to perform the sacred task of self-criticism, particularly when it strays from its God-given calling. Rabbi Greenberg argues that modernity and modern values, in particular democracy and pluralism, have helped Christianity and Judaism enter into a purifying process of self-criticism. He believes that Islam, located mainly in countries where the Islamic religion dominates exclusively, has a greater distance to go in fostering the necessary self-criticism. For Rabbi Greenberg, then, the key question is how to bring democracy into religion without weakening religious authority.

> To reduce their violent tendencies, all religions must now take upon themselves the commitment to a thoroughgoing radical pluralism. Religions should insist on pluralism in religious life, and in economic, political, and social life, as well as in culture, to protect against their own totalizing tendencies. Religions can lead the way in taking up the risks involved in sustaining an atmosphere in which every faith and all kinds of lifestyles are available. The risk is that the unrestrained marketplace of ideas and values can lead to a condition of cultural relativism in which no values stand up. The potential gain is that faiths learn to witness effectively in the presence of the full dignity of the other.

Judaism, he continues, draws upon three fundamental dignities of the image of God: first, people are created in God's image and therefore have infinite value; second, all people being made in God's image makes all people equal; and third, all people are unique—not even identical twins are identical. All people bear an obligation to save the lives of others. But our world is not ideal, and war as self-defense may be necessary. The use of force in self-defense is not the same as violence. In the meantime, Jews should commit themselves to perfecting the world, to the work of *tikkun olam,* so that the use of force is not needed.

His Eminence the Grand Mufti of Bosnia-Herzegovina, Dr. Mustafa Ceric, emphasized his European and Muslim identity, the contribution of Muslims to Western Civilization, and the historical roots of Islam in Europe. He discussed the Bosnian genocide, rejecting the notion that extremists represent Islam. His presentation, titled "Judaism, Christianity, Islam: Hope or Fear of Our Times," drew attention to the great Muslim thinkers who in the fourteenth century laid the foundation for religious freedom that supported not only basic human rights, but also genuine forms of democracy. Citing the texts of the Qur'an that forbade any compulsion in religion and affirmed the value of religious pluralism, Dr. Ceric expressed regret that so few modern Muslim intellectuals have built upon this rich late medieval foundation. Affirming that a human being is neither like God nor like an animal, Dr. Ceric explained: "Man is too ignorant to be allowed to carry out God's final inquisition, he is too meek to hold God's power, and he is too selfish to maintain God's full justice. And man cannot be an image of an animal because he has a heart and mind. Man is too precious to God to be an object of Holocaust, he is too proud to be ethnically cleansed, and he is too intelligent to allow the law of the jungle to prevail." Dr. Ceric concluded his address by returning to two doctrinal and historical Islamic principles: no compulsion in religion and the universal declaration of equal rights that the prophet Muhammad delivered at one of his ceremonies on the hill of Arafat: "You are all children of Adam, and Adam is from clay. Let there be no superiority of an Arab over a non-Arab, nor a non-Arab over an Arab, and neither shall there be superiority of a white over a black person, or a black over a white person, except by good character."

In his turn, Charles Taylor chose to describe the sources of violence. He searched for an explanation of "categorical violence," a special sort of violence directed at groups or categories of people. He dismissed as inadequate explanations given by sociobiology or attributions of violence to testosterone, and proceeded to examine the issue of meaning, or the metaphysical roots of violence. Drawing on the thought of René Girard, he described how certain forms of violence ensured purity for the perpetrators and created a contrast between them and the "others," who often were made into scapegoats. Some forms of violence even take on a "sacred" form.

Professor Taylor argues that by the time of the French revolution, murder had become more efficient through the use of the guillotine. A republic presupposes a form of popular sovereignty that makes it difficult for minorities who, if not assimilated, become threats to the majority. Modern political identities make ethnic cleansing possible. Violence against categorical identities is now one of the most pressing dangers in the twenty-first century.

Taylor concluded his reflections by agreeing with Immanuel Kant, who argued that ordered democratic societies are more likely to be less violent, especially if they learn to spread their benefits. Nevertheless, in our own day, religion and secular humanism have their own distinctive "viruses." In the long term, the most effective response to violence may well be religions that recommend forgiveness and acknowledge that all humanity, including both majorities and minorities, is flawed.

At the end of the first day, all three speakers sat before the conference participants and commented on each other's presentation and responded to questions from the floor. Candid exchanges, especially between Rabbi Greenberg and Dr. Ceric, revealed differences yet to be resolved, not so much in the actual potential of each one's religion to be a force for peace, but in their respective understandings of the consequences of the political settings in which their co-religionists lived.

EXAMINING INDIVIDUAL RELIGIOUS TRADITIONS

On the second day, three scholars, one representing each religious tradition, explored the resources in their tradition for justice and peacemaking. Rabbi Reuven Firestone examined both Biblical and Talmudic sources, beginning with Exodus 15:3, which calls God a "God of war," and describes Israel as boasting that it destroyed every man, woman, and child of the communities they opposed. In contrast to this text, Rabbi Firestone looks at several texts that teach peace and reconciliation. How are these very different texts to be understood? Which indicate what is truly at the heart of Israel?

Rabbi Firestone argues that it is most important to keep in mind that the Hebrew Bible is not Judaism, nor is Judaism the Hebrew Bible. What exists today is rabbinic Judaism, a form of the Jewish religion that took shape at about the same time as Christianity itself began. For the Jews of today, the Talmud, that is, the "oral Torah," parallels in sanctity and importance the written Torah, that is, what Christians commonly call the Old Testament. More important, one finds very little written about war in rabbinic Judaism. In fact, in all of this massive body of literature, only one paragraph is devoted to war. It distinguishes between commanded and discretionary war. Why so very little about war? Because, according to Firestone, it was too dangerous for the Jews to write more—they had no political, much less military, power. Since the destruction of Jerusalem by the Romans in the first century, Jews have been "quietistic," a historical necessity that caused some Jews to understand their religion, naively, as morally superior to the religions of the Gentiles.

All this changed, however, with the birth of the State of Israel in 1948. Nearly twenty years later, during the six-day war of 1967, the Israeli forces not only doubled the state's territory but also "captured almost all the villages, cities, and valleys that are mentioned in the Bible." In view of such a conquest, one orthodox Jew declared that the war represented "another stage on the way to our Redemption." And in view of his belief that God had worked a miraculous conquest, then it followed that they were "not free to return even one handful of land," for they possessed a "legal promissory document regarding it in the Torah." In the face of such a dramatic change from "quietistic" Judaism to the military victory of the army of Israel, Rabbi Firestone concludes his reflections by asking: "Does this mean that we must abandon religion altogether to be moral?" In 1999 he published *Jihad: The Origin of Holy War in Islam* (Oxford); he is currently working on a book on the idea of the holy war as it appears in Judaism.

Scott Appleby, Professor of History and John M. Regan Jr. Director of the Joan B. Kroc Institute for International Peace Studies, University of Notre Dame, devoted most of his address to describing the profound shift within Christianity, and especially within Catholicism, that has taken place in the last fifty years. He states his thesis at the outset: "I will argue that a momentum has been developing, both within Christian theology and praxis, toward nonviolence as the heart of the Christian ethic, to the point where today it is seen by significant numbers of Roman Catholics, main-line Protestants, and, of course, by members of the historic peace churches, not merely as an option but as the nonnegotiable dimension of Christian discipleship."

After examining briefly and then refuting six typical ways to explain away the nonviolent example of the person and life of Jesus, Professor Appleby begins to spell out a growing consensus of thinkers and movements that support his thesis. The key turning point for the Catholic Church was its declaration on religious freedom issued by the Second Vatican Council (1962–65). Through that document, the Church dropped earlier claims to political privilege, gave up its theocratic model of political order, and "became a powerful proponent of religious liberty and universal human rights." Appleby sketches the evolution of the major themes of Catholic social teachings, beginning with Pope Leo XIII's 1891 encyclical *Rerum Novarum,* strengthened by Pope John XXIII (1958–63) and Vatican II, and then further developed by liberation theology.

If the Catholic Church now defends religious freedom, what happens to its traditional great commission from the Lord to go forth and make disciples of all nations (Mt. 28:19)? Appleby takes up this question in his conclusion, in which he describes the great shift in how the Church has come to understand its missionary responsibilities. The Gospel of Jesus Christ is best proclaimed by the promotion of human rights, religious freedom, and a genuine respect for other religions.

Finally, Professor Mohamed Fathi Osman, of the Institute for the Study of the Role of Islam in the Contemporary World at the Omar Ibn Al Khattab Foundation, opened his presentation by citing numerous texts of the Qur'an that made clear God's will that all humankind is called to peace, that human life should not be destroyed and that evil should be repelled with good. In other words, within the Qur'an one finds ample texts to provide a solid foundation for going beyond violence. All human beings enjoy an inherent dignity bestowed by God. Citing again the Qur'an, Osman explains that human diversity should neither be ignored nor stopped, but should be a basis for "competing" with other religionists in doing good works. Like Dr. Ceric, Professor Osman draws attention to the important text that states that in matters of religion, there is to be no compulsion. Finally, he cites texts that state that Muslims should never initiate war. Even in acts of self-defense, they should return to peace whenever it is offered.

In the light of all these texts, Osman then asks the obvious question: What has gone wrong? He is currently engaged in writing a lengthy book explaining how to interpret still other texts of the Qur'an that may be used to support war and violence. He argues that a thorough look into the particular text itself, especially when it is considered in context and combined with other Qur'anic texts, and within the Qur'an in its entirety, would not give any support to violence. In his address, Osman chronicled the misuse and misunderstandings of "jihad," which led to certain schools of Islamic jurisprudence that supported the idea of constant war as a means of spreading Islam. This aggressive trend grew even more widespread when confronted with European colonialism. Many Muslims, Osman concludes (though he admits that he somewhat oversimplifies these trends), thought in modern times that "sticking to the juristic heritage about 'power'—not the 'moral' power that is the essence of faith in God and is always supportive and productive, but the 'physical' power—and about universal confrontation would let them pass the present with all its weakness and humiliation and restore the past with all its glories."

Part of the problem facing Muslims today, Osman believes, is learning how to deal with sacred sources. More specifically, Muslim scholars need to develop criteria by which they can distinguish permanent divine principles from others, on the one hand, and be merely enlightened but not bound by human elaborations on and derivations from them and from texts, on the other. Once such rules of interpretation are established, then Muslims can distinguish between texts that are merely descriptive historically and those that are permanently normative. In summary, Osman states that Muslims today face three major challenges: the impact of colonialism followed by the current domination of the West; the polarization between certain forms of Muslim militancy and modernization; and the hermeneutic problems of interpreting correctly sacred texts. He concludes with a plea not just for Muslim leaders, but for all religious leaders, to work together to move beyond violence, and more specifically, to take up the challenges of both peacemaking in the midst of violence and scholarship that will make the Islamic religious foundations for that sacred work clear and compelling.

At the beginning of this introduction, I mentioned that interreligious dialogue is really only in its infancy. But even very small children can give some indication of the types of persons they eventually will become. This conference represented just such an early stage in interreligious dialogue. Nevertheless, certain family resemblances could already be seen. First, all three religions face the difficulty of focusing on the circulating interpretations of their texts, some of which have been used to support violence against others, sometimes against fellow religionists and more often against those of other religions. Since the Holocaust, Christians have become painfully aware of the ways in which certain New Testament texts have been used as a basis for anti-Semitic thoughts and deeds. Texts of the Old Testament, as made clear in Rabbi Firestone's presentation, show clearly that at one time in the history of the Jewish people, war, and not just defensive war, was considered holy. And recent terrorist events and wars in the Persian Gulf, Afghanistan, and Iraq have drawn attention to texts in the Qur'an that seem to legitimate violence and to their authoritative interpretation. Religious leaders and scholars of all three traditions need to devote themselves to addressing the proper interpretation and character of such texts for believers today, particularly by attending to their historical and scriptural contexts.

Second, the discipline of interreligious dialogue includes not only intellectual, but also emotional and personal, dimensions. That there are deep hurts, both historically sustained by a tradition and personally absorbed by individuals, becomes clear when interreligious dialogue is honest. The pain must be acknowledged, and even embraced, worked through and not worked around, if it is ever to be transformed into energy for reconciliation. Not only does such transformation take time, but it requires support from those who have already made that difficult journey. It also requires facing the "other," and discerning in that person a humanity that until then remains an abstraction of evil.

Third, and finally, as important as interreligious dialogue is, it may well be the case that even more important is the formation of friendships with people of other religions. When there is friendship, there is respect and the desire to be even-handed when criticism and plaudits are offered. Friends realize that truth, uttered without sensitivity to the time or the context, can harm. The letter to the Ephesians exhorts Christians to speak the truth in love. Archbishop Rowan Williams recently wrote: "Truth makes love possible; love makes truth bearable."[4]

The four individuals who spent the better part of a year organizing this conference experienced this simple but profound truth of the important relationship between friendship and dialogue, love and truth. No sooner had the conference ended than all four agreed enthusiastically to continue to work together on still other projects. Perhaps our own interreligious dialogue has moved beyond its infancy.

NOTES

1. "Clergy Confab Examines Religion's Role in Conflict," in *Cleveland Plain Dealer,* May 3, 2003, an article by Karen R. Long. This statement by Turner has been frequently repeated by veteran historian of American religion Martin Marty, who is featured in the article.

2. See Samuel Huntington, *The Clash of Civilizations and the Remaking of World Order* (New York: Simon & Schuster, 1996).

3. Kenneth Woodward, "Graham's Crusade: Should Evangelicals Invade Iraq?" *Commonweal,* June 6, 2003, 9.

4. Rowan Williams, *Open to Judgment* (Darton, Longman and Todd, 2002), cited in the *Tablet,* February 15, 2003, 29.

1

Notes on the Sources of Violence: Perennial and Modern

Charles Taylor

THE ENIGMA OF VIOLENCE

What I want to focus on here is not violence in all its aspects, which includes domestic violence, criminal violence, and the like. What concerns me is categorial violence, exercised against whole categories of others, people therefore that one may never have known or been in contact with. I'm thinking of the violence wrought against a scapegoat minority or phenomena such as ethnic cleansing or genocide. And, needless to say, the events of September 11, 2001, come very much to mind.

The fact that these events recur so frequently in our "civilized" century is deeply troubling. How can we explain this recurrence? Is it a mere survival, a throwback to earlier times? What is deeply disturbing about this violence is not just that it occurs at all, that people can be motivated to kill whole categories of others, often on patently irrational grounds, but also (1) that this violence is frequently excessive, spreading beyond its original target to englobe more victims or involving atrocities and mutilations; (2) that it can involve some language of purification, as one sees with a term such as *ethnic cleansing;* and (3) that it can also include a ritual element. These latter two features remind us sometimes of modes of violence that belong to sacrifice in primitive religions, and this can enhance the sense of a throwback.

One way of explaining the recurrence of violence would be to offer an explanation on the biological level, since this presumably

remains the same in human life, even as culture "advances." We note
that men, even more frequently young men, are usually the perpetrators, and that can point us to a hormonal explanation. Does it all
come down to testosterone? But this seems radically insufficient. It
is not that body chemistry is not a crucial factor; however, it never
operates alone in human life, but only through the meanings things
have for us. The hormonal explanation does not tell us why people are susceptible to certain meanings. It could at best explain
the brute fact of violence, for instance, whenever we're crossed.
Thus, men are more violent in relationships than women. But even
that is questionable considering the findings, such as those of James
Gilligan, that humiliation is an important causal factor in individual violence.[1]

Now forms of group violence seem to have very complex meanings, which often have to be understood on the level of the whole
culture. There is the business of designating the enemy; not to speak
of the phenomena of excess, purification, and ritual, as mentioned
above. These seem to demand understanding in cultural terms, and
indeed, their forms differ from culture to culture.

This is what makes the sociobiological explanations, which
attempt to account for the continuing recurrence of these patterns,
so unsatisfactory. They offer an account in quite general, acul-
tural terms: positing, for instance, that people have learned to be
aggressive to outsiders and to bond with insiders. We can see how
such behavior might have had an evolutionary payoff. But this kind
of account makes the "meaning" here irrelevant, unless it be simply an instrumental-rational reflection. But, quite the contrary, the
meanings invoked are not only crucial, but they tend to be metaphysical; that is, they raise questions, or are answers to questions,
about such concepts as the meaningfulness of life, good and evil,
and moral integrity.

My aim is to identify some of these meanings. Excess, purification, and ritual seem to point back to "primitive" history, religious
history, and indeed, "primitive" religion. Are these phenomena mere
throwbacks? Yes and no. There is a continuity with this history, but
it is more like a new edition of an old story or the transfer of old
melodies to a new register.

THE METAPHYSICAL MEANINGS OF VIOLENCE

How should we understand the higher significance, the metaphysical meanings of violence?

As far back as we can look, we see that religion often involves sacrifice in some fashion or other. We need to give up something; it can be to placate God or to feed God or to get His favor. But this demand can also be spiritualized or moralized: we are radically imperfect, below what God wants. So we need to sacrifice the bad parts, or sacrifice something in punishment for the bad parts.

The sense of unworthiness plays an important role here. But humans have also always been under threat from destructive forces. There are fierce hurricanes, earthquakes, famines, floods. And then also in human affairs, there are wildly destructive people and actions: invasions, sackings, conquests, massacres. Or perhaps we feel the menace of ultimate entropy.

It may be that these are given a meaning by being subsumed into the terrible demands of baleful fate, which is ours in virtue of what we owe to the gods or of our imperfections. This account fits the Nietzschean idea that we want to give a meaning to suffering in order to make it bearable. But we could also see it the other way around: the sense of lack, of our falling short, is the primitive factor; and we need to give a shape to it. Not: first suffering, then we look for a meaning, so suffering becomes punishment; but: first deserving punishment (or the sense of falling short), so we look for certain modes of suffering to give a shape to all this, or a sense of how we can make it up. So our punishment becomes identified with this suffering. In this way, even natural destructive forces come to be seen as wild and full of a spirit of destruction.

Religion can thus mean that we identify with these demands or fates. So we see destruction as also divine, as with Kali-Shiva. And when you can bring yourself to identify with it, you are renouncing all the things that get destroyed, purifying yourself. Wild destruction is given a meaning and a purpose. In a sense it is domesticated, becomes less fearful in one way, even as it acquires part of the terror of the numinous.

This of course involves submitting to an external, higher will, purpose, or demand; it requires decentering. But there is also a way of dealing with violence and destruction, and the terrible fears they arouse in us, which gives us a sense of power, of being in control. It is a central part of the warrior ethic. We face down the fear of destruction; we accept the possibility of violent death. We even see ourselves as, in advance, already claimed by death: we are "dead men on leave." Think of the symbolism in naming a regiment after the death's head: the Totenkopf battalion of the Prussian army.

Then we live in the element of violence, but like kings, unafraid, as agents of pure action, dealing death; we are the rulers of death. What was terrifying before is now exciting, exhilarating; we're on a high. It gives a sense to our lives. This is what it means to transcend. In the words of Sudhir Kakar, commenting on his interviews with leaders of the communal riots in Hyderabad: "The excitement of violence becomes the biggest confirmation that one is physically still alive, a confirmation of one's very existence."[2]

We can see in all warrior cultures how this willingness to risk life is a source of dignity; it is a crucial basis of honor. Those who flinch are dishonored (the basis of the dueling code). We see this reflected in Hegel's Master-Slave dialectic: both sides in the duel to the death wish to prove that they have set themselves above mere life.[3]

Honor in turn intensifies the drive to vendetta. We lose face unless we pay back fully in kind what has been inflicted on us.[4] Hence one way of dealing with the terror stills the turbulence of violence, either depriving it of its numinous power or identifying it with some higher such power, which is ultimately benign. The other keeps the numinous force of violence but reverses the field of fear; what previously made us cower now exhilarates; we now live by it, transcend normal limits through it. This is what animates battle rage, berserker fury, which makes possible feats of arms undreamed of in our everyday mode.

There are also ways of combining these two responses, as in some cultures that practice human sacrifice. On one hand, we submit to the god to whom we offer our blood; but the sacrificers also become agents of violence. They do it instead of just submitting to it. They wade in blood and gore, but now with sacred intent. Because it combines the two strategies for dealing with this terror, there is nothing more satisfying than a sacred massacre. René Girard has explored this terrain, where religion and violence meet, in a series of path-breaking works.[5]

Girard sees sacred violence as that of a people finding unanimity again in an attack on a victim. This heals the rifts of mimetic rivalry, which otherwise threaten to tear them apart. This is part of the mechanism of sacred violence. But there seem also to be other dimensions; there are:

(a) The offering of some part of our goods to God, in order to conserve the rest, such as Aztec sacrifices to the God of the corn. The numinous dimension enters here with the sense of being fed by the God, spirit, totem, or whatever; then there is the sense that we need to be worthy of this, or to win favor for this. We need to give, and this has to cost us. So—sacrifice.

(b) The raising of violence to the level of the sacred, making it a way of participating in the power of God, participating in the divine destruction. So we purify ourselves of what seems evil, or merely self-absorbed, in our aggression. This may play a part in ritual sacrifice, but also in the Girardian mechanism of expelling the scapegoat.

(c) But then this latter expelling violence also purifies, because it is a way of affirming its presupposition, viz., that that which is expelled, or the enemy, concentrates all evil in itself. It is no longer in us, but outside us.

PURITY AND CONTRAST

But how does this get focused? How do some people become targets?

We find one account in (1) the mechanism of sacrifice, as described by René Girard. First there is mimetic rivalry, which threatens to dissolve our society; then we forge a unity out of everyone-minus-one, the victim; and this restores the general peace, but at the expense of the person sacrificed. But this is not necessarily extensionally equivalent to (2) the scapegoat mechanism. Here there is a catharsis, expelling evil, with the corollary that what has been expelled concentrates all evil in itself. Again we give vent to a holy rage.

The second approach also shores up unity, but against another danger, the sense that the order that binds us is suffering corruption, breakdown, loss of solidity, or of a really firm allegiance.

This sense of our solidity can also be achieved (3) by focusing on an external enemy. War is deep in human history. Keegan[6] argues that first it too was largely ritualized. This limited the damage. The irony is that "progress" has meant greater destruction, because of "rational" action. There can also be mimetic rivalry between societies, as with nineteenth-century imperialism.

How do we understand (2) above? Why do we want to purify or expel evil? And how do people become candidates for the scapegoat role? Who becomes the outsider? We define ourselves in terms of our beliefs, ethic, ideal order, or way of life. We need something like this, because we cannot just live with chaos: evil, violence, wrong, destruction, desert, and meaninglessness. We saw this above, in our manner of dealing with destructive forces. But we also cope by holding evil to be outside. Seeing oneself as evil, or in moral chaos, disables, paralyzes. We cannot admit it, or else we reverse the field and say something like "evil be thou my good," or we go "beyond good and evil," like Nietzsche.

To see the evil or disorder as external, we need a contrast case. The role has been played by "barbarians" and "savages." Of course the contrast case can be distant, people with whom there is no real contact. The contrast helps define us, but also defines evil, failing, lapse, as outside. At least we're not savages, barbarians, Nazis, Stalinists, robbers, murderers, child molesters, and so on.

Where there is no contact this can be relatively harmless, although it can license terrible cruelty on contact. Think of the conquista, the slave trade, the way that they released the joys of aggression. But then there are also cases in which the outsider, the contrast case, can be seen as a vital threat. One way this can happen is that the enemy can be within.

This can be (a) because we're tempted, as with some homophobia or myths of the sexual potency of outsiders. Or else (b) the order is under some kind of strain. Then the Girardian scapegoat mechanism defines the outsiders as operating inside; they are polluters. This is typical, for instance, of mediaeval European anti-Semitism. This kind of thing happened frequently in the enchanted world. The witchcraft craze, another striking example, came at a boundary between the two ages, as disenchantment was under way.

Of course, (a) and (b) can combine. But also (c) the boundary may tend to erode. Emancipation, and the end of the enchanted age, undermined the old sense of a boundary around Christendom.

All these factors come together in the late nineteenth and early twentieth centuries to create a terrible new anti-Semitism. This was motivated by envy and a felt threat to order that seeks a scapegoat, but at the same time there was also an eroding of the boundary. Because of emancipation, the Jews were no longer outsiders in the same sense, so that the "enemy" was within. This culminates in Nazism, which brought together a renewed warrior ethic, reversing the field of fear and taboo, and mobilized a scapegoat attack, complete with the mythology of expelling evil: holy rage, sacred massacre.

SACRED KILLING

We can perhaps understand the scapegoat mechanism as a convergence point between two formations. One is the response of assuring ourselves that we are good and ordered by identifying a contrast case from which we separate ourselves. We draw the line between us. This can be expressed in terms of purity and pollution, the self-affirming contrast. The second is the strength and spiritual force that come from identifying with numinous violence, the violence of the gods—identifying actively, in some form of sacred massacre. We can have the self-affirming contrast without the sacred massacre, for example, the Indian caste system. But when they come together, the result is peculiarly powerful.

This sacred killing powered by the contrast comes in two major forms, if this rather oversimplified grid can be imposed on a host of complex phenomena. There is the scapegoat mechanism as such, wherein we turn on, kill, or expel an outsider (contrast case) who is within, who has eroded the boundary. And then there is the crusade, wherein we go to war with a contrast case outside. The latter, in addition to fusing together numinous violence and purity, also realizes another powerful synthesis: it bonds the warrior stance, as lord of death, with the higher cause of numinous violence. So it both gathers all this

potentially centrifugal violence into a higher unity and also gives the
warrior self-affirmation a higher meaning and purpose. The Crusades
are a paradigm case, a "solution" to the grinding conflict between
Christian faith and the aristocratic-warrior way of life of the rulers of
medieval society, to the perpetual battle of the Church to impose a
"peace of God" on an unruly and bellicose nobility.

What is involved in identifying with numinous violence? This does
not mean necessarily identifying with the good. In the preaxial period,
the gods were both benign and malign, some mainly one, some mainly
the other, most often both. "Benign" here is measured in relation to
ordinary human flourishing: life, health, prosperity, many descendants.
We have often to trick and propitiate these higher beings (hence the
importance of the "trickster" figure). But the axial revolution tended
to place the divine on the side of the ultimate good, while at the same
time redefining this as something that goes beyond what is understood as ordinary human flourishing: nirvana, eternal life.

Some forms of the axial transformation bring God closer to a
conception of morality, some code that is justified and made sense
of in terms of this higher good, as with Plato. We also see this with
the God invoked by the prophets, who frequently enjoins us to forget sacrifice and succor the widows and orphans.

In an important sense, the modern disengaged rational and secular world goes even farther in this direction. Morality rationalizes.
That is, the code is based on a conception of what the good or right
is, related to human well-being. This brings with it a notion of responsibility. We punish wrongdoers. We move away from the ambivalences
of early religion, where the sacred brought both boon and danger,
where we can worship the victim of the sacrifice afterward.

In the Christian context, identifying with divine violence became
identifying with the (of course, righteous) wrath of God. And so we
persecute heretics. Also witchcraft trials participate formally in this
logic, however based on murderous fantasies. The modern moral
order, and the disenchanted, rationalized world, should put an end
to all this. There is no place for the wrath of God, and even among
believers there has been a "decline of hell." But as we see with anti-
Semitism, it can intensify evil. Of course, we could argue that this
may just be a transition: see the situation of Jews in the contemporary United States and in much of Western world.

But moralizing may make things worse, and the question arises whether we do not invent new murderous fantasies in the enlightened, disenchanted world. How "dated" is this violence, precisely the "excess"? Note how in the modern world, the original sacrifice of victims, who are both sacred and dangerous, sources of trouble and of healing, is broken apart. This yields (a) the scapegoat who is entirely wrong, evil, as in witchcraft or anti-Semitism, and (b) the purely righteous sacrifice: the brave young men fallen in battle, an idea ultimately derived from Christianity.[7]

Let's now look at some of the modes of this transition to new forms of categorial violence.

PATRIA O (Y) MUERTE

First, let us look at the democratic republic. We are citizens together, ruling as a people. A certain narration is inseparable from this. We can see how often this narrative is violent. It speaks of the violence done to us and our good counterviolence. This latter often bears the name of *revolution*. Well, we might say, here is no myth. That is history. We had to fight. Violence *was* done to us. True. But does that explain the whole thing?

Let us look at the French Revolution, and its ultimate filiation with the (Castrist) slogan *Patria o muerte*. This is a tradition that englobes Jacobins, then Bolsheviks. But first we should examine the link between democracy and violence: the Terror.

What is the Terror? Not just violence against enemies. There were real enemies, inner and outer. But beyond what can be explained by these there was first (1) the fabrication of enemies, who did not need to be seen as such. All those who disagree are seen as traitors, as irremediably hostile, to be eliminated; these included all people of certain classes, regardless of their actual stance. The violence therefore escalates. A similar extension of hostility to whole categories explains the genocidal policy in *la Vendée*. Then we see (2) the discourse surrounding this; it is a discourse of purification: getting rid of impurities, poisons. This goes along with a language of virtue, of the purity of the republic. Then thirdly, there was (3) the quasi-ritual element: public executions.

The Terror can be understood in two perspectives. First, it is a hangover, a continuation. Its source was the culture of popular rebellion in the ancien régime. The people in cities could rise against abuses such as engrossing *(accaparer),* price gouging, when the price of corn rose steeply. These actions reflected a strong community code, what Edward Thompson has called the "moral economy."[8] The sense was that, when things go wrong, someone is to blame. The people could not accept that the impersonal mechanisms of new political economy were the problem. They had to find a villain, either the *accapareur* or perhaps some corrupt royal official. And having identified the evildoer, they exercised a kind of violence against him, going all the way from purely symbolic acts, like burning in effigy, through the destruction of property, to terrible forms of execution. This punishment, whatever it was, was seen as a kind of retribution/purification.[9]

There is no doubt that this popular culture was pushing the assembly and convention throughout the early years of the revolution. Particularly traumatic for the political élites of the Constituent Assembly and the convention were the frightening popular massacres of September 1792. There seemed no other recourse but to attempt to canalize this violence; simply suppressing it seemed out of the question. As Danton put it a year later in the autumn of 1793: "Soyons terribles pour dispenser le peuple de l'être." This in turn created a climate in which the temptation inevitably arose to win every factional struggle by mobilizing this mass sentiment against one's adversaries; but this meant turning the factional struggle into a fight for life. It was a Hobbesian world, in which attack was sometimes the only form of defense, and the attempt to stop the spiral of killings could be fatal, as Danton learned to his cost.

Second, there is a perspective that stresses the ideology of virtue and purity. This was clearest with Robespierre. For Robespierre, the key to a republican form of government was virtue, defined in a somewhat traditional way as "l'amour exclusif des lois de la patrie." But this in turn was given a Rousseauian gloss: virtue exists when love of self and love of one's country are fused together in one. "L'âme de la République, c'est la vertu, c'est l'amour de la patrie, le dévouement magnanime qui confond tous les intérêts dans l'intérêt général," as he put in in a speech of 1792.[10] In the face of this ideal, all those who fail to rise to these heights, all the "lâches égoïstes" are enemies of the republic. From this it is just a step further to conclude that the new form can really come into being only when those enemies have been removed from the scene. For "l'esclave de l'avarice ou de l'ambition pourrait-il immoler son idole à la patrie?" This removal would constitute a purification. The high goal thus sought would justify the most stringent means for it would finally "remplir les vœux de la nature, accomplir les destinées de l'humanité, tenir les promesses de la philosophie, absoudre la Providence du long règne du crime de la tyrannie" (from a speech of February 5, 1794).[11] And in fact, the paroxysm of Terror in June-July 1794 was based on this idea of killing to purify, to bring about a reign of virtue.

This philosophy had certain disquieting parallels to the outlook underlying popular revolt. First, all evils were attributable to evildoing. There was no question of explaining certain of the ills of the new society by impersonal factors, deep divergences of interest, or effects of scale. If things were going wrong, there had to be a "plot." The constant reference to a "complot aristocratique" was what united this popular culture and the Jacobin discourse. And the link between the two was forged by agitators like Marat, who kept the public in a state of febrile vigilance against hidden enemies. It followed second, that those responsible for our misfortunes were actuated by ill will; they were vicious and incorrigible. The republic of virtue could come about only through their purgation. Eliminating them was a purification of society.

Now in fact, I want to argue that both these perspectives are right. The parties of the revolutionary élite were forced into the politics of the Terror by popular pressure and the irresistible temptation that this provided to win over their adversaries through an alliance with the mobilized sections. This in turn gave a place to the Jacobin discourse that it would never have gained on its own, in a struggle with other ideological tendencies unaffected by the pressure from below. But the result of all this was the re-editing of a new form of purificatory violence at the heart of "rational" modernity. The Jacobins tried to channel popular revolt, but they also tried to rationalize and purify it. It would be justified not just by a traditional morality, but by a rational outlook on virtue, moreover one that promised to lift the condition of humankind to a new plane. By the same token, the victims were to be selected by rational criteria and not just the instinct of the mob. And the new liturgy of purification was "clean" and scientific, the swift and surgical death by guillotine, as against the cruel play of symbolism of the vengeful crowd, which mixed elements of carnival hilarity with those of gruesome spectacle. The old melody of scapegoat stigma and purification was replayed in a new register of rational morality. One can argue that Bolsheviks later follow a similar path.

We feel a paradox here: the ideal is a republic of perfect equality, justice, peace—the most ordered and peaceful regime in history. So how can it treat humanity as an impurity to be purged? Robespierre incarnates the paradox. He voted against the death penalty during the debates of the Constituent Assembly, which was designing the future constitution. These two sides of the revolution have to be brought together. The very idea of high moral purity involved in the true republic means that those who knowingly, willfully refuse it must be truly evil. They are incomprehensible (as real evil is); they are not really human. They are to be likened to animals. (This latter idea was, indeed, built into the natural law doctrine, as articulated, say, by Locke, who says that those who violate it may be treated like lions and tigers). And so finally, those who stand in the way are total enemies, irrevocable enemies, to be simply eliminated. So royalists and foreigners are enemies. And the enemies of the Republic are "immondices," and "rebuts de l'humanité."[12]

Thus unity was achieved through the purgation of inner enemies (scapegoat mechanism). But we can also attain this unity and purity through the defeat of external enemies (crusade). These two can be linked. Indeed, it became possible to appease the mechanisms of inner purgation through the common cause of the fight with the coalition. This is what the directory was trying to do. Napoleon realized this at its fullest. The sacred war, the crusade, was the spreading of the revolution to Europe. But this also subsumes the warrior culture of the ancien régime; and the value of glory on the battlefield was now democratized with the career open to talents.

We can see analogous meanings in the American Civil War. For the abolitionists, one had to purge the evil of slavery. Civil war allowed them to make the inner purge an external one. But we also see the idea of having to atone for sin being invoked in Lincoln's second inaugural address.

The revolution overcame its inner divisions by a sublimation of the temptation to inner purgation through the glorification of external war/crusade. This is what makes the cult of sacrifice, of the noble dead, so central to the new republican identity. We see a parallel sublimation in republican historiography, which attempts partly or largely to disculpate Robespierre because of "circumstances," that is, the fight against enemies, the coalition and La Vendée, passing over in silence what is really troubling in the Terror: our three elements of excess, purification, and ritual.

Part of the legacy of this revolution in modern democracy is that the very heart of much patriotism, what gives it a higher dimension, what bonds us to something great, noble, unbreakable, is the memory of the people united in (holy) war. We can't break with the dead; we must keep faith with those who have sacrificed their lives for us. So—"sacrifice" again, and "tombs" and the "sacred." We are bound by the dead. (Benedict Anderson has written very tellingly on this.) This democratization of the cult of dead warrior heroes is consecrated in the tombs of the Unknown Soldier. This cult can partly account for the ease with which modern, rational, "civilized" Europe sleepwalked into the hecatomb of the First World War, and thus incurred the massive destabilization that followed for Western civilization. Destabilization seems connected to the democratic state. But it also mutates into nationalism.

NATIONS AND CLEANSING

The republic supposes a new agency: the people or nation. The nation can be conceived as a previously existing cultural and linguistic entity. The nation is different from other nations, but this difference is unlike that between what we formerly understood as religious communities or civilizations. The nation is supposedly one among equal others. This notion of one among others even survives the metastasis of fascism, minus the recognition of equality. But the idea still is: this way is only for us. What is jettisoned is the universalism.

The nation is founded on "will," like the republic. But this in turn appeals to "identity." The modern horizon is described in terms of the contemporary notion of "identity." Identities, unlike the fixed horizons in which premoderns moved, (a) are one among many, and (b) need to be defined, further determined. On the individual level, (b) holds because of the ethic of authenticity, the idea that each human being, or each group, has its own way of being human. On the social level, (b) holds largely because of the sense that either (1) we have never really had our moment; our identity has been suppressed by some intolerant majority or some rapacious empire, and/or (2) as history changes, we have to redefine ourselves to continue our authentic form of life. We have to tell our story in a way that culminates in today's identity. Hence all the bad, "invented" history of which Hobsbawm speaks.[13]

Identity goes together with recognition. The new horizon has to be defined; and so a lack of recognition can derail us at a very profound level. The more powerful and more successful have a unique power; their gaze can disturb, devastate, hamper the identity definition of those less secure—and the more so in that we are frequently divided about what our identity consists in.

Now given that a nation, an identity, is one among others, why does this not solve the problem? Can we not all learn to tolerate each other? This may be hard because following "our" way, and being able to do so, becomes all the more important in our age. It is our way of being human in the modern world. And this may be destabilized from outside by a lack of recognition or a crass misrecognition.

But the tensions are also intensified by democracy, or sovereignty based on popular will, which requires a political identity. We have to be on our own, in order to live out our way; and we cannot be challenged by others who might want to dispute the legitimacy of that way.

This tension is increased by our attachment to a specific territory, which is an essential feature of the modern state. Our identity becomes linked to this land. The peculiar nature of modern identities is that, although they are always the result of creative redefinition, they are also linked to a given, be it language or tradition, but also soil, and sometimes also religion, as a historic marker.[14]

In this context, others become an identity threat. This is a form of the threat to the integrity of our social order that was discussed above and that has been occurring since time out of mind. But this is of a new kind and in an unprecedented context. The context is that of popular sovereignty (popsov), which may make it impossible to live with a minority as a safe, subordinate population, for instance, as *dhimmis* were under the Caliphate. They are a legitimacy challenge and hence an identity threat. Under the principle of popsov, the political identity of a state must be ultimately decided by the people. But if we include this minority in our "people," they may easily vote to change our political identity; if we exclude them, then we deny them one of the recognized rights of modernity, that of citizenship in a sovereign people. In either case, they may want to dismember our territory. So we have to assimilate them, or else when they remain refractory, we are tempted to ethnically cleanse them. This is why the twentieth century has been both the age of rising democracy and the heyday of ethnic cleansing. This is not a mere coincidence.[15]

We feel an analogous painful paradox to the one that arises around the Terror. Since the enframing idea of modern nationalism is that each people is one among others, that everybody has a right to be, how can we exclude others like this, much less kill them? Because by being here, they are aggressors. Here's where the benign context itself turns malignant. The benign context is that all peoples have a right to their identity. Where something goes wrong and this picture can't be carried out, it is because there is some aggression by some against others; some are depriving others. We can't live our identity fully on "our" territory, so we're being prevented by those who stand in our way. They are the aggressors; hence, we are victims.

The framework of equal peoples is the basis for the universal appeal to the victim scenario today. This is a remarkable fact about our age. Where my identity is being blocked, this must be because I am being unfairly put upon—unfair in the light of the ideal order of equal, coexisting identities. We are victims, underdogs.

We can see how the modern moral order intensifies the conflict by moralizing it. Take the bad old days when we faced aggressive outsiders, say, in the Balkans, where Christians faced Muslims. The Muslims are our traditional enemies. On top of that they have embraced an incomprehensibly perverse form of religion. On both

these grounds, it is "normal" that they attack us and we defend ourselves. It is part of the order of things; they can't do other than attack,
under either description. No hard feelings, in a sense.

But now in the modern universalist moral understanding, they
are equal participants in the same moral order, which they have violated, while we are innocent. They are in something of the category
that a renegade from our side might have been in under the old dis-
pensation. They have read themselves out of the protections of the
order. They are bad, evil; they have the worst coming to them. And
fighting them is a way of giving expression to our innocence. Modern morality gives the cachet to the victim scenario.

There is a double moralization here: first, rights are violated;
second, democracy or popular sovereignty itself is more highly
moralized; it requires self-responsible action; it calls forth duty.
Modern moralizing ups the ante; it gives group hatred a new charge
of holy rage. Hence Communists who can wipe out kulaks. And
now this is transposed to certain older rivalries with different peoples in the Balkans.

So we hate these people as aggressors. Take the Muslims in India,
in the eyes of the BJP: we can burn down their mosque, because it
is taken to be a fruit of aggression. Among less sophisticated members of the party the discourse becomes very crude: Muslims don't
belong here; send them to Pakistan. So the framework of popular
sovereignty and coexisting equal peoples can generate its own grounds
for hate and even killing. Thus our paradox. Note how much of this
framework even the Nazis took over: negating the universal order,
of course, but inheriting a particular identity. They then played extensively on the sense of grievance. Germany was unfairly blamed for
the war and, before that, unfairly denied its place in the sun. Hitler
railed against the "Diktat" of Versailles. He invoked the "stab in
the back." Let us purge the traitorous elements, invoking holy anger.

The logic is: we have been unfairly treated, so we can strike
out. Unfair treatment is invoked by most terrorist movements today.
We see lots of it today in Palestine, and not just on one side.

Note the terrible alchemy: How does an identity threat become
a mortal threat? A minority can be an identity threat by just being
there. So this threat is turned first into an act of aggression. But wanting to wipe us out as a political identity is close to wanting to wipe

us out tout court. We just need some believable atrocity stories. But there are always men, often young, who are ready to act out aggression and violence, as discussed above. So atrocities are committed. Some group cleanses village A; then a countergroup cleanses village B. Then we have believable atrocity stories to tell on both sides. The mechanisms of vendetta take over. What is tragic here is the terrible destruction of trust, even where people have lived together for years and intermarried. And then the tragic situation spirals downward.

This situation must also be put in the context where elites are trying to recruit the masses to their concern with nation or identity. Provoking massacre can further this enterprise. And so we have Bosnia in the 1990s or the Punjab (1947). But the recent history of the Punjab, wherein the killing between Sikhs and Hindus seems to have come to an end, shows that this terrible dialectic is not irresistible. Sometimes the fabric of cross-community relations can win out over the attempts to destroy it by massacre.

What I'm suggesting here is that nationalist violence can be put in the broader category of violence generated by the threat surrounding modern collective identities. In this context, we can see the analogies with movements like El Qaeda, in which the sense of threat is mobilized around, not a nation or a language, but an idealized Islam, supposedly undermined or attacked by "Jews and Christians," or by America. And it is understandable that in what we often class as "nationalist" movements, the main marker of difference can be a "religious" one, as with the BJP in India.

The move of modern history has been toward a wider and wider recruitment of people into such identities from out of earlier, more local identifications, focusing often on kinship systems, clans, or tribes. These early identities are often defined by "networks," in which people stand in a dense web of relations, linked to many people but in a different fashion to each one, as in a kinship system, where I am related to one person as father, another as son, another as cousin, and so on. In contrast, modern political identities are "categorial"—they bind people together in virtue of their falling together under a category, such as Serb or American or Hindu, wherein we all relate in a uniform way to a whole.[16]

This movement seems to be accelerating. Many factors are drawing people away from the earlier network identities—not only the efforts of élites to mobilize them, but also migration, or the effects of globalization, either through the spread of media or the undermining of older ways in which we make our living. Migration can mean being mixed with unfamiliar others, not knowing how they will react, being unable to reconstitute the older way of life. Loss of the older forms of making a living can undermine our dignity, our identity; it can induce a sense of loss and helplessness. The decay of the old often brings disorientation or feelings of humiliation and lowered self-worth.

In these circumstances, a new categorial identity can offer people something very precious: not only a direction, an orientation, but also a sense of (collective) agency. We are no longer just to suffer a sense of helplessness before dimly understood global forces, but we are to be mobilized against named and identified ills. It is not surprising, in the light of what I said above about scapegoating and holy wars, that these ills are often attributed to a source in an enemy, who wants to destroy us and whom we must combat. We should measure how overwhelming the temptation can be to go along with this kind of (often murderous) mobilization when it comes across as the only way to recover orientation, dignity, agency.[17]

Violence around categorial identities is one of the most pressing dangers of the coming century. It could literally destroy our world.

MORALLY DRIVEN HATE/EXCLUSION

I have been dealing with what we all recognize as the terrible cases of group violence. But along with this, we have in the modern world highly peaceful societies, where the level of everyday violence is quite low. Indeed, in some of these societies, the level is very much lower than in earlier epochs. Compare France under the ancien régime and the France of today, for instance. So modern civilization presents the paradoxical spectacle of societies that, in their "normal" internal operation, sometimes through long periods are more pacific than any others in history, while at moments at their boundaries, so to speak, they wage hugely destructive wars, which can then in certain circumstances engulf them, and on occasion they can even fall prey to civil wars. If we look only at the long periods of internal peace, we can nourish the hope that modern civilization will tame war and violence, which is one of the great aspirations of liberalism. If we think of the terrible destruction of modern war and ethnic cleansing, we are plunged into gloom.

But how does it work when it works? Our civilization is built on an idea of order between equal, rights-bearing individuals, whose action should be directed to mutually enriching and mutually enhancing forms of self-realization. This is not just an idea, but also something that has become entrenched in the institutions and practices, political and economic, in the social imagination, and in the disciplined training of modern subjects. As an established order, it does a great part of the time succeed in keeping us in line and preventing the worst of mutual violence and threats, though we sense how fragile this order can be, and in particular how much depends on the inclusion of masses of people within the mutually enhancing mechanisms of the economy and welfare state.

But even when it works at its best, the modern order can secrete various forms of contempt and exclusion, which replicate some of the motives that break out in violence in less restrained contexts. In the earlier sections, I was dealing with the survival of full-blooded violence, sometimes highly ritualized, always with a purificatory element. But there is also subviolent hatred, even where violence is contained. Let us look at some of these.

Consider another facet of the modern moral order: many of the disciplines that constitute it, as well as the intellectual outlook it inculcates, call for an objectifying, disengaged stance—one that seems consonant with a "scientific" perspective. This justifies itself for a host of reasons, but not least because it separates us from the wild and metaphysical-religious sense of the numinous power of violence and sexuality. It thus should preserve us from going along with holy anger. And it also allows us to see calmly and coolly what needs to be done. We can become calm, collected, clear-seeing agents of healing, of reform, of betterment.

Objectification easily goes along with the therapeutic stance. When we come to treat our problem cases, we are dealing not with evil but with different kinds of pathology, which we have to heal. We seem at the antipodes of Robespierre, with his pervasive moralization. But the therapeutic perspective justifies us in dealing with these people as charges, patients. Evil has a certain dignity, that of deep investment in a distorted vision of the good. Pathology is just incapacity. Such thinking is the source of a potentially paradoxical deviation, in which a benign stance turns malign.

This deviation can also be seen from another side. The disengaged stance is also a distancing strategy. Thinking of these people as sick, pathological, needing therapy makes them other, not real interlocutors, not really embodying alternative possibilities that can draw us, tempt us. So there is an analogue here to the earlier mode of identifying the outsider as a contrast case, as another species, as savage. Outsiders exist in another space, behind a turn in the road, where they aren't our interlocutors. But their not being real interlocutors, fully responsible beings, also can mean that you can treat them roughly, even perhaps that you have to. You want to make them shape up. We don't need to be too tender with them. See how the politically correct in the United States treat those classed as "homophobes" or "misogynists." We can use shaming as an instrument of coercion or compulsory reeducation or worse.

The benignity of disculpation can become the malignity of rough, contemptuous treatment. But perhaps also something worse is happening. Perhaps that holy anger is recurring here. So one distancing strategy can become the cover for another, much older one. Dostoyevsky has given a penetrating depiction of this turn, for instance, in *The Possessed*. Disengagement can become partly a sham, a comedy we play with and on ourselves.

The two kinds of hate—identity driven and liberal-moral driven (or Jacobin- or Bolshevik-moral driven)—can combine, that is, in the crusade of our civilization against Milosevic's Serbia. My invoking this example does not mean that I think the policy was wrong. That is another, and very difficult and complex, issue. But right or wrong, we should be clear about the kinds of feeling mobilized behind it in our societies. And some of these are troubling.

In a quite different and, one might say, even opposite way, this distancing, disengaged stance encouraged by the modern moral order can generate violence, by reacting to it. There is an attempt in our modern liberal world to work directly against the mechanisms I have been describing in the previous sections, to take all the numinousness out of violence, and make life tame and ordered. This means also leveling down the hero. From almost the beginning, this reaction has provoked another reaction to what is seen as a leveling down of life, a denial of heroism and greatness. The denial of violence is also that of warrior dignity, and this has seemed to many too high a price to pay. Perhaps the most influential figure who has given voice to this reaction, and in one of the most radical forms, is Friedrich Nietzsche. His influence is ubiquitous in the higher culture of the last century. And this kind of reaction has also erupted onto the political scene, with fascism. It goes on today without benefit of either high culture or fascist ideology in outbreaks of violence by, for example, skinheads.[18]

LE SOUCI DE LA VICTIME

The defeat of the Nazis left room for another powerful narrative. This is what Girard has called "le souci de la victime."[19] This shows the tremendous force of the New Testament in our culture. But this impact is also captured and deflected.

There is a narrative of the modern world, like and parallel to that of the growth of freedom, democracy, which sees us as redressing all the historical wrongs and inequalities. We rescue and recognize all the victims. But this is connected to the moralism of meting out punishment to perpetrators, victimizers—which justifies wreaking punishment and vengeance on them. So another powerful engine of destruction is born, and an equally paradoxical one.

The concern for the victim is, in Girard's view, the religion, an absolute of the modern world. How should we understand this? Partly in terms of the modern moral order—but this is not sufficient. This provides the standard of equality and mutual respect, against which victims are identified. But there is something more in *le souci de la victime*.

This more is the idea that we move toward the ultimate order through the unmasking of hidden victimizations, which are covered up, denied, and have to be denounced. So it is part of the dynamic theory of how we move toward the order, not prescribed by the order itself, which was after all originally used for the justification of the established structures, or what underlay these structures, the proper constitution of power, as for instance, with Locke.

This concern is a more direct borrowing from Christianity. The Gospel involves a reversal, showing the victim to be innocent; it points toward the raising up of victims, of the despised and rejected. Various religious reforms involve taking this idea of reversal farther. The Reformation itself is one such example, as also is modern humanism, which defends ordinary human life against persecution in the name of "higher" modes of spirituality.

So this élan becomes part of the ethic of our time, the political ethic. Joined to a view of history, this yields a transfigured version of the modern moral order as eschatological idea. This becomes on one hand, a great force for battling against injustices. But it also becomes a way of drawing lines, denouncing enemies, the evil ones.

Hence comes the powerful cachet of victimhood. This would have been very surprising to our ancestors living by the warrior ethic; no Greek warrior would insist that he was the oppressed serf. Friedrich Nietzsche would be doubly horrified. Why this cachet? Because my being the victim means that you are the victimizer. I am pure. Claiming victimhood is an assertion of our purity; we are all right. Moreover, our cause is good, so we can fight, inflict a violence that is righteous: a holy violence. Hence we have a right to do terrible things, which others have not. Here is the logic of modern terrorism. Even the Nazis made use of a proto-form of this: "I have suffered terribly at the hands of others; therefore I can wreak mayhem."

All such thinking depends on the external placing of evil and therefore on a dichotomizing of good and evil. Now according to the outlook of modern disengaged objectification, we are not supposed to believe in evil. But this is subverted by the fact that the very definition of ourselves as people of good will seems to require that we see the others as evil. So we show our goodness in fighting against the bad guys.

Even for the greatest disenchanters, evil has to return to their picture, because they have a sense of themselves as actuated by a pure, good will, and have to see, somewhere their opponent, pure evil. So there are new myths of evil, which are not admitted to be such theoretically. They have to fit the myths of good will. These are Rousseauian: we are all good au fond. So whence comes evil? Bad upbringing, perhaps, or being abused. But this reduces the agents of bad to victims themselves, people who have become incapacitated. The therapeutic perspective dominates. Somewhere we need to find an object to expel, one which concentrates evil. At first, this can just be the "system," as remarked by David Martin.[20] But the search for evil needs in the end wills. So it alights on those who support the system. These are the really evil people, the real victimizers, even though they may be hiding this from themselves; they may not realize it; they may think the system totally "normal"; even so, perhaps especially so, they are the evil ones. They can be treated as pure enemies.

Vanquishing Violence

Does all this tell us anything about how to lessen violence or get rid of it? Have we a hope of doing this? Let us consider first what I will call the Kant hypothesis, although he was not the only person to hold this view. This is the idea that ordered, democratic societies will become less violent; they will not go to war with each other and presumably will not suffer civil wars. There is some truth to this, as we saw above. Modern disciplined order has had some effect. But the peace is fragile, for a host of reasons—partly because there are certain success conditions of economic order, partly because of tensions of exclusion and rivalry that remain subviolent but generate hostility. And then there is the problem that some societies have great trouble acceding to the category of ordered democratic polities.

So any program to overcome violence must contain at least two objectives: (1) build such ordered democratic polities; (2) try to make their benefits spread as wide as possible, for example, by preventing the formation of desperate, excluded groups—particularly young men.

But this program seems radically incomplete in the face of the carryover or, better, re-editing of older forms of scapegoating and holy war to our day. Can we do something to fight these? Is there a third element to our program?

One answer might be: let us note the metaphysical and religious roots of this categorial, purificatory violence. So, how do we get rid of it? It is religious, or at least metaphysical, and so we will get rid of it only by totally overcoming the religious dimension in our existence. The problem up to now is that many of the main builders of a supposedly secular republic, the Lenins and the Robespierres, have not really liberated themselves from this incubus as they thought they had.

But it seems clear from the phenomena reviewed above that just proposing some nonreligious theory, such as modern humanism, does not really do the trick. The religious forms seem to reconstitute themselves. So we would have to fight for a real, thoroughgoing disenchantment, a total escape from religion. How do we do this? Is this really possible?

This suggests another answer: all the above shows that the religious dimension is inescapable. Perhaps there is only the choice between good and bad religion. Now there is good religion. For instance, there is Girard's take on Old and New Testaments, as the source for a counterstory to the scapegoat narrative, which shows the victim to be innocent. And we can say something analogous about the Buddha, for instance.

Thus we can point to the Gospel picture of a Christian counterviolence: a transformation of the energy that usually goes into scapegoat purification, transformation that reaches to overcome the fear of violence not by becoming lord of it, by directing it as an annihilating force against evil, but that aims rather to overcome fear by offering oneself to it, responding with love and forgiveness, thereby tapping a source of goodness and healing.

But an analogous point to the one just made about humanism can be made about these religious positions. Just adopting some religion, even a, in principle, "good" one, does not do the trick. Christianity is responsible for *le souci de la victime* in the modern world. But we see how this can be colonized by the religion of purification of scapegoats. Do we want to protest that this is a secularized variant? Then how about the long, dreary, and terrible history of Christian anti-Semitism? Seen in a Girardian light, this is a straight betrayal of the Gospel, a 180-degree reversal. Just believing in these "good" religions does not overcome the danger. Both sides have the virus and must fight against it.

Where does this leave us in our search for a third kind of measure in our program? We noticed a pattern in the paradoxical reversals above. The goodness that inhabits our goal, or our vision of order, is somehow undone when it comes to struggling to realize it. Robespierre's republic without a death penalty somehow energizes a program of escalating butchery. Similar things can be said for the Herderian order of nations coexisting in diversity or the goal of rescuing all victims. The paradox is that the very goodness of the goal defines us, its builders and defenders, as good and hence opens the way to our grounding our self-integrity on a contrast case who must be as evil as we are virtuous. The higher the morality, the more vicious the hatred and hence destruction we can, indeed, must wreak. When the crusade comes to its fullness in the moralism of the modern world, even the last vestiges of chivalric respect for an enemy, as in the days of Saladin and Richard Coeur de Lion, have disappeared. There is nothing left but the grim, relentless struggle against evil.

There is no general remedy against this self-righteous reconstitution of the categorizations of violence, the lines drawn between the good and evil ones that permit the most terrible atrocities. But there can be moves, always within a given context, whereby someone renounces the right conferred by suffering, the right of the innocent to punish the guilty, of the victim to purge the victimizer. The move is the very opposite of the instinctive defense of our righteousness. It is a move that can be called forgiveness, but at a deeper level, it is based on a recognition of common, flawed humanity.

In Dostoyevsky's *Possessed*, the slogan of the scientific revolutionaries who would remake the world is "no one is to blame." That is the slogan of the disengaged stance to reality, of the therapeutic outlook. What this slogan hides is another stance that projects the blame entirely on the enemy, giving ourselves the power to act that comes from total righteousness. Opposed to this is the insight that Dostoyevsky's potentially redemptive characters struggle to: "we are all to blame." It is this restoration of a common ground that defines the kind of move I am talking about. It opens a new footing of co-responsibility to the erstwhile enemy.

It is best to see this in an example. And a very remarkable example stands in our recent history. I am thinking of Nelson Mandela. There was great political wisdom there. Following the only too understandable path of revenge would have made it impossible to build a new, democratic society. It is this reflection that has pushed many leaders after periods of civil war in history to offer amnesties. But there was more than that here. Amnesties have the flaw that they usually involve suppressing the truth or at least consciousness of the terrible wrongs that have been done, which therefore fester in the body politic. Mandela's answer was the Truth and Reconciliation Commission, one that is meant to bring terrible deeds to light but not necessarily in a context of retribution. Moreover, the deeds to be brought to light were not only those of the former ruling side. Here is the new ground of co-responsibility that this commission offered.

No one knows if this will ultimately work. A move like this goes against the utterly understandable desire for revenge by those who have suffered, as well as all the reflexes of self-righteousness. But without this forgiveness, and even more, the extraordinary stance of Mandela from his first release from prison, what I have called his renunciation of the rights of victimhood, the new South Africa might never have even begun to emerge from the temptations to civil war that threatened and are not yet quite stilled.[21]

There are other examples in this whole field of transitions from despotic and often murderous régimes, inseparable from the spread of democracy. The Polish case also comes to mind, as well as the strong advice of people like Adam Michnik to forego the satisfactions of retribution in the name of building a new society. The Dalai Lama's response to Chinese oppression in Tibet offers another striking case.

It is in moves of this kind that we need to seek the third element in our program. They follow neither of the lines suggested above in that, although they clearly derive a lot from the religious traditions involved, they are not necessarily the fruit of a personal religious faith. But however motivated, their power lies not in suppressing the madness of violent categorization, but in transfiguring it in the name of a new kind of common world.

NOTES

1. James Gilligan, *Violence* (New York: Vintage, 1996).

2. Sudhir Kakar, *The Colors of Violence: Cultural Identities, Religion, and Conflict* (Chicago: University of Chicago Press, 1996), 81.

3. See the importance of "Daransetzen": "Und es ist allein das Daransetzen des Lebens, wodurch die Freiheit, wodurch es bewährt wird, dass dem Selbstbewusstsein nicht das *Sein,* nicht die *unmittelbare* Weise, wie es auftritt, nicht sein Versenktsein in die Ausbreitung des Lebens das Wesen—sondern das an ihm nichts vorhanden, was für es nicht verschwindendes Moment wäre, das es nur reines *Fürsichsein* ist." *Die Phänomenologie des Geistes* (Hamburg: Felix Meiner Verlag, 1952), 144.

4. This interweaving of the warrior code of honor, the vendetta, and sacred violence, is evident in the Palestine-Israel conflict. It emerges also in this telling quote from a leader in the communal riots in Hyderabad: "Riots are like one-day cricket matches where the killings are the runs. You have to score at least one more than the opposing team. The whole honor of your nation (*quam*) depends on not scoring less than the opponent" (from Sudhir Kakar, *The Colors of Violence,* 57).

5. See among others *Le Bouc émissaire* (Paris: Grasset, 1982) and the more recent *Je vois Satan tomber comme l'éclair* (Paris: Grasset, 1999).

6. John Keegan, *A History of Warfare* (London: Hutchinson, 1993).

7. It is in this context that I would like to understand the thesis about monotheism and violence of Regina Schwartz's interesting and suggestive work, *The Curse of Cain* (Chicago: University of Chicago Press, 1997). I am suggesting that the phenomenon is perhaps more widespread and general than she proposes.

8. E. P. Thompson, "The Moral Economy of the English Crowd in the Eighteenth Century," *Past and Present* 50 (1971), 76–136.

9. See Albert Soboul, "Violences collectives et rapports sociaux: Les foules révolutionnaires" in *La Révolution française* (Paris: Gallimard, 1981), 577–78; and François Furet and Denis Richet, *La Révolution française* (Paris: Hachette Pluriel, 1999), 206–7. The idea that someone must always be to blame for catastrophic events is, of course, common in many "primitive" cultures; see, for instance, E. E. Evans-Pritchard, *Witchcraft, Oracles and Magic among the Azande* (Oxford: Clarendon, 1937).

10. Cité par Georges Lefebvre, in *Quatre-Vingts-neuf* (Paris: Éditions Sociales, 1970), 245–46.

11. From Patrice Gueniffey, *La Politique de la Terreur* (Paris: Fayard, 2000), 311–13. I have drawn a great deal on the interesting discussion in this book.

12. See again Gueniffey, *La Politique de la Terreur,* 310. He shows the same demonization of opposition in the case of the mass killings in La Vendée. The people here were described as animals, dehumanized as a preparation for massacre. There is a continuity with the prerevolutionary language of élites describing the people (255–61).

13. Eric Hobsbawm, *Nations and Nationalism since 1780* (New York: Cambridge University Press, 1992).

14. I have described elsewhere how religion slides to becoming a marker for identity. See *Transit,* published by IWM, Vienna, volume 15, 1996.

15. I have discussed this drive to exclusion at greater length in "Democratic Exclusion (and Its Remedies?)" in *Multiculturalism, Liberalism and Democracy,* ed. Rajeev Bhargava, Amiya Kumar Bagchi, and R. Sudarshan (New Delhi: Oxford University Press, 1999), 138–63.

16. See Craig Calhoun, for instance, his "Nationalism and Ethnicity" in *American Review of Sociology* 9 (1993), 230. The discussion in this section owes a great deal to Calhoun's recent work.

17. I have learned a great deal from the interesting discussion in Sudhir Kakar, *The Colors of Violence,* especially chapter 6.

18. I have discussed this at greater length in "The Immanent Counter-Enlightenment," in *Canadian Political Philosophy,* ed. Ronald Beiner and Wayne Norman (Don Mills: Oxford University Press, 2001), 386–400.

19. See *Je vois Satan,* chapter 13.

20. D. A. Martin, *Dilemmas of Contemporary Religion* (New York: St. Martin's Press, 1978), 94.

21. For an interesting discussion of the advantages and dangers of a truth commission of this kind, see Rajeev Bhargava, "Restoring Decency to Barbaric Societies," in Robert Rotberg and Dennis Thompson, eds., *Truth and Justice* (Princeton: Princeton University Press, 2000), 45–67.

2

Judaism, Christianity, Islam: Hope or Fear of Our Times

Mustafa Ceric

"The evil we are talking about here was not committed by Christians, but by those who have broken all the teachings of Jesus. Those who have raped women and killed innocent people have no religion. They are simply murderers."[1] I wish Alija Izetbegovic was able to come personally to this conference and read you this and many other of his statements concerning his understanding of religion and morality in the context of world affairs of today.

Unfortunately, his age and health did not allow him to be with you today in Los Angeles. He has asked me to represent him and to convey to you his warm salams, or greetings, and sincere thanks for giving him the Omar Ibn Al Khattab Distinguished Pathfinders Award for his contribution to "visionary leadership and magnificently distinguished service to Bosnia, Islam, and humanity" and for your interest in his ideas about the role of religion in today's world.

I am sure you are familiar with his work *Islam between East and West,* in which he tried to explain the role of religious morality in the context of the time of communism, hoping for Islam to be an avant-garde in promoting the morality in politics that would lead to a moral as well as political reform of society.

In the meantime, President Izetbegovic, has published other works[2] that are more autobiographical than religious in their form and content, but certainly they express his moral and political opinions concerning both national and international issues of our times. Having experienced the time of totalitarianism, President Izetbegovic is a strong advocate of fair and balanced democracy, free thought and speech, for he believed that only free men can assume moral responsibility. This, in turn, led him to the belief that only free and democratic Muslim societies can be morally strong and politically wise. In addition to that, Izetbegovic believes that a good education on all levels is the best way for Muslims to earn the rightly deserved respect of the global community.

Needless to say, I hold the same views, but I must admit that I am not able to present to you fully what Alija Izetbegovic really is in the richness of his Islamic morality and in the greatness of his political thought. However, I have humbly accepted his request and your kind invitation to come to this honorable conference with a sincere desire to share with you our Bosnian experience, which is both painful and hopeful in our search for truth, justice, peace, and reconciliation. Therefore, I am pleased and honored by Izetbegovic's choice to represent him here today and by the kind invitation of my dear brother Dr. Mahmoud M. Dakhil to witness your goodwill that is represented in such highly esteemed religious dignitaries and scholars.

The United States of America is the mightiest nation in the world today. It has a historic chance to become the greatest nation in modern history as well. Hence, it is worthy of mention here that for someone to be big and mighty does not necessary imply that he is equally great and always right. He will, however, be both great and right by promoting truth, justice, and freedom, the values that are dear to each person and every nation on our planet regardless of his or her or its religion, nationality, race, or color. This is what we, the small nations, hope for: that the big nation does not fail to be great and that the mighty does not forget to stand right. And this is exactly what I am pleased about here because I see Omar Ibn Al Khattab Foundation, the University of Southern California, Hebrew Union College-Jewish Institute of Religion, and the Institute for Advanced Catholic Studies coming together to discuss the ways that will lead all of us to the greatness of our faith in One God who created us out of a single substance and made our world rich in the diversity of our physical and spiritual being.

It is with that idea in mind that I have chosen for my presentation on this occasion the title *Judaism, Christianity, Islam: Hope or Fear of Our Times,* hoping that I will be able to highlight a long-felt need for the children of Adam and Eve and the spiritual offspring of Nuh, Ibrahim, Musa, Isa, and Muhammad (peace be upon all of them) to recognize the fact of their common spiritual roots, so much so that there is no religious source of their own that can be properly understood without referring to the source of the other. While reading the Holy Qur'an, a Muslim cannot but feel in almost every page of it the presence of the People of Book *(Ahlu-l-kitab)*. By the same token the Jews and Christians cannot read any relevant book of the world history without recognition of the Muslim presence in all fields of human life.

Sure, the Qur'an criticizes some Jews and Christians, but it does the same with some Muslims as well. It is the Muslim moral responsibility not to take advantage of the critique of others in the Holy Qur'an in order to cover the Muslims' own shortcomings. If nothing else, because the Qur'an, as the word of God, is almost unique in appreciating the goodness of people of other religions, especially of the *Yahud* and *Nasara,* the Muslims have a duty to carry out the spirit of tolerance in the midst of religious pluralism. Here is one of many verses of the Holy Qur'an that clearly indicates that fact: "Verily, those who have attained to faith (in this divine writ), as well as those who follow the Jewish faith, and the Christians, and Sabians[3]— all who believe in God and the Last Day and do righteous deeds-shall have their reward with their Sustainer; and no fear need they have, and neither shall they grieve" (2:62).

Of course, it would be naive to conclude that there are no differences between Islam and other religions and, more specifically, between Islam on the one hand and Judaism and Christianity on the other. The point here is not a vague notion of poor flattering or cheap religious propaganda, but a sincere conviction based on the most important Islamic source that teaches Muslims how to cope with religious pluralism of their own and how to appreciate the fact that this world is not made up of one religion or one nation. For if God wanted the world to be so, He could make it so. Rather, He wanted the people of this world to be multiple in their religions and nations so that they may compete with each other in good deeds.

This idea of the competition in good deeds applies, especially, to these three world religions of the Book—Judaism, Christianity, and Islam—not only because of their claim to the similar heritage of the Book, but also because of their heritage of a unique historical interaction that could not be avoided in the past and their historical responsibility that cannot be ignored in the future. It is precisely in this historical unavoidability of Judaism, Christianity, and Islam that I see hope, but also, I must say, I sense a kind of fear. My hope is based on the good heart of the majority, though very often silent in its goodness, of sincere Jews, Christians, and Muslims who seek their own peace in the similarity of these religions rather than in conflict among them.

Unfortunately, there is a very loud minority in all three religions who, in fact, see in the similarity of Judaism, Christianity, and Islam the very reason for conflict rather than peace. This kind of attitude leads us almost to the conclusion that the similarity, and not the difference, provokes the conflict while the difference brings the respect. We are familiar with the history of a severe debate among the similar, not different, religious groups, the debate that has often turned into a very violent conflict. I have in mind some historical conflicts between the Sunnites and the Shiites in the Muslim religion and the conflict between the Catholics and Protestants in the case of Christianity. I am sure that such examples exist in Judaism as well.

The logic of this kind of conflict among those who are similar, whatever it may be, lies in the false notion that in order for me to keep the purity of my religion, the deep difference must be seen of the other who is similar to me, but, at the same time, his difference is not tolerated. This is, I believe, the real issue of the relationship between Judaism, Christianity, and Islam today: their similarity, not the difference in their spiritual roots; their hope, not the fear from each other; their love, not the hate of each other; and their justice toward each other, and not the oppression of each other.

Of course, I can speak on behalf of Muslims and say that we have all the more reason to remind the Jews and Christians of our similarities because we are told over and over again in the Qur'an and the Sunnah that Moses was a great prophet, while Jesus was the prophet of God who was raised up to heaven almost at the beginning of his mission (Muslims believe that Jesus was not crucified). The Muslims may disagree with Jews and Christians, but they should not show disrespect for the prophets *of Tawrat* and *Injil*.

Unfortunately, as Stephen Schwartz has observed, Muhammad has an evil reputation among Westerners that sets him apart from Moses and Jesus. Jews and Christians reject Muhammad as the apostle of a religion they fear. Jews deny that Jesus was Messiah, but many among them have come to recognize him as a great religious teacher. Little such respect has been accorded to Muhammad. Rather, the Arabian prophet has been treated with contempt, both by Jews, who have tended to ignore him, and by Christians, who load his name with insults. Islam is considered by most Westerners a hideous, bloodthirsty, intolerant, and aggressive cult, and Muhammad himself has been widely portrayed by non-Muslims as devious, brutal, and perverted. Jews carried away by outrage have fostered bestial images of Muslims. Equally biased Christians have denied that the God worshipped by Muhammad and his followers is the same as the God of Jews and Christians.[4]

I have cited this statement of Schwartz in order to show, once again, that the difficulty in our relations is not the difference, but similarity. You will notice, for example, that the above-mentioned attitudes toward the Prophet of Islam would be almost impossible to hold toward Confucius or Buddha, because they are different and it is not difficult for us to respect their way of religion. In the spirit of our similarity, then, I would like to proceed and to remind you that the Bible says, "In the beginning, was the Word";[5] that the Qur'an asserts, "In the end will be the Word of God";[6] and that in the middle is man, hopeful to know the beginnings and fearful to meet the ends.

Would man's knowledge about the beginning improve his behavior in the middle and would his prophecies about the end make him responsible for what he says and does in the middle of all things around him? Will a common road from cosmogony to eschatology of Judaism, Christianity, and Islam lead humanity to a middle path of decent ethics and morality?

One thing is for sure: man is not eligible to know the beginning of the first creation, simply because he was not witness to the creation of the heavens and the earth, nor of the creation of his own self (Qur'an, 18:51). The same goes to his prophecies: man is not entrusted to tell when and how the end of the world should be because he is too selfish to afford the continuity of the creation after his personal departure (Qur'an, 79:42).

Instead, man is invited to have faith in the word of God and remember that the moment Adam and Eve had tasted the apple, the human story of disobedience and courage began. Their disobedience has been condemned and their courage glorified. Those who see Adam and Eve's disobedience only increase human guilt; and those who see their courage only increase human arrogance. Adam and Eve are guilty because they had broken the law; they are arrogant because they had tasted the knowledge.

Consequently, Adam and Eve had to leave the peaceful garden and come to the turbulent Earth that is full of hope for their success, but also contingent with fear from their failure. Only, now they realized the significance of law and the risk of knowledge. Their repentance for disobedience has been accepted, and their courageous adventure has been inherited. It became too late for them to go back to the garden by their knowledge alone. They had been told that they ought to earn the garden back by faith in God Almighty and by trust in the Law of His Word.

The Adam—man—and the Eve—woman—have been constantly reminded by Nuh (Noah), Ibrahim (Abraham), Musa (Moses), Isa (Jesus), and by Muhammad (peace be upon all of them) that God is with them as long as they listen to God's guidance. They have been told not to listen to the whispering of Iblis (Satan) because he is among their worst enemies.

By Noah they were supposed to learn the necessity of building the Ark for human salvation; by Abraham they have been taught how to distinguish true God from false gods; by Moses they should have appreciated the power of law in the face of injustice; by Jesus they might have discovered the love in suffering. And by Muhammad (peace be upon all the prophets) they have been told that the secret of success in this world is in truth and justice.

Of course, man and woman have never entirely denied God's guidance. Yet they have never fully accepted it. They often wanted to lead their lives as if there were no God. Yet again they thought themselves to be like God. They liked the idea of human beings as the image of God, as if there had been no other creatures as beautiful as him or her, if God needs any image at all. It is man's desire to see himself like the image of God or to deny God altogether that led him to "taste the apple" once again. This time, his falling from the heat of the image of God to the cold reality of animal was, indeed, a big event; almost like Adam and Eve's fall from the Garden of Eden. Man was happy by the new knowledge of his beginning. He thought that he had finally freed himself from the heavy lightning of the image of God to the enlightenment of the image of his own mind. He has celebrated his new time and looked to his bright future on his own. He felt no need to apologize to anyone for taking the image of an animal, not even to monkeys, which might wonder how is it that humans want to be like monkeys. But sadly we can see that it is less probable that some monkeys become men than for some men to become monkeys in the sense of their lack of decent and responsible behavior.

However, the more man stayed in the cold reality of the world of animals, the sooner he realized how difficult it is to be like an animal. Why? It is because man is neither like God, nor is he like an animal. Man is simply like man. He is comparable only with himself. God is not comparable with anything, the least with man who likes to be like an animal. Man cannot be an image of God because he cannot be God to judge the man as God's creature. Man is too ignorant to be allowed to carry out God's final inquisition; he is too meek to hold God's power; and he is too selfish to maintain God's full justice. And man cannot be an image of an animal because he has his heart and mind. Man is too precious to God to be an object of holocaust; he is too proud to be ethnically cleansed; and he is too intelligent to allow the law of the jungle to prevail.

Hence, both according to the Bible and the Qur'an, two things we can learn from the story of Adam and Eve: first, the man's desire for eternity and his longing for a kingdom that never decays; and, second, his fear to meet the end of the things he has made to stay beyond the termination of his life on the Earth. We have plenty of examples of their desires: from the ancient time of the pyramids to the modern time of huge towers in major cities around the world.

It is, then, in his desire to be remembered and in his fear to be forgotten, that man is impatient to regain the lost eternity of Adam and is unhappy to see the end of his garden of influence on the Earth. But once again, here and now in the garden of Earth, something like a ghost is whispering to man: "Atomic weapons and the weapons of mass destruction shall lead thee to the tree of eternity and to a kingdom that never decays."

Can Adam and Eve this time avoid the seduction of the evil voice of Satan, or are they ever destined to make the same mistakes? Is

there any place left for Adam and Eve to run away from the garden of Earth with their sins? Can Adam and Eve win over the fear
and fulfill the desire of humanity for eternity that is beyond the end
of our temporal stay? Is humanity at the end of its history that promises a new beginning, or is it at the beginning of the end of its ever-
hoped-for liberty, equality, and fraternity?

To the historian Ibn Kathir al-Qurashi al-Dimashqi (d. 1373) the
history had the beginning and the end during his lifetime, so he
wrote the book of *al-Bidayah wa el-Nihayah* (The Beginning and the
End).[7] No, Ibn Kathir did not mean to inform us about the end of
history, but rather to indicate that as far as he is concerned, history
ends at his departure from the garden of Earth; the rest of it he leaves
to God.

It is not unusual that some religious men who have been deeply
concerned about the destiny of humanity announce from time to
time the end of the world because of their impatience against the
temporal imperfections. In fact, it was considered that religion is the
only source for such announcements as the end of the world. Perhaps, in order to remove this kind of unpleasant reminder, Dom
Aelred Graham came with an idea in 1971 to tell us about *The End
of Religion*.[8] He explains how it has been thought by some that
science will take the place of religion and that we will then feel safe
from the fear of any kind of ends, at least the one that religion is
frightening us from.

To his disappointment, however, John Horgan tells us that we are
at *The End of Science*[9] and that because we face the limits of our
knowledge in the twilight of the scientific age, we have to go back
to some kind of religion, reminding us of the prediction of almost
forgotten German philosopher Spengler, who observed in *The Decline
of the West,* "As scientists become more arrogant and less tolerant
of other belief systems, notably religious ones, society will rebel
against science and embrace religious fundamentalism and other irrational systems of belief." Spengler predicted that "the decline of science and the resurgence of irrationality would begin at the end of
millennium."[10]

After the assumed end of religion and the suspected end of science, what else can one expect from Francis Fukuyama than for him
to declare *The End of History and the Last Man?*[11] Fukuyama is not

afflicted with the religious pessimism of the medieval sort. This is the scholarly sophisticated mind of the modern man who sees the end of history because he cannot comprehend the world beyond his scholarly possessed ideas, as if he really possesses them for himself and for his own lifetime only. Fortunately, man does not possess the ideas. He only chooses them as they fit his particular needs or beliefs.

The same goes with the new "prophet" of the modern time Samuel Huntington, who sees the new world in the context of *The Clash of Civilizations and the Remaking of World Order*. It is not only that these two cannot go together—the clash of civilizations and the world order—but that these ideas cannot go with a sound mind of any order whatsoever.

Therefore, I tend to agree with John Lukacs that we are *At the End of an Age*[12] of scientific shortcomings and historical untruths. We are entering, or we are supposed to be entering, a new area in search for a new meaning of religion and culture, of science and history—indeed of a world order that will not end with an atomic blast or with weapons of mass destruction, but will begin with moral must and human trust that will enable our children to remember us and not to forget us forever.

If dreaming is free of charge, without which dreaming there is no change, then let us have a dream that the wise man from the East, if he still exists, and the rational man of the West, if he still thinks, hail the moral man of the Earth, who can bear the moral must and hold fast to the human trust in the future of our world that is made to be for many tribes and nations so that they may know each other better. Why? Because I believe that neither the meek nor the aggressive will inherit the Earth, but only those who cooperate in truth, justice, peace, and reconciliation among people and nations.

Therefore, we should not allow that the already passed road of humanity be reverted from freedom to slavery, nor allow that bright science be swallowed by dark mythology, nor that the noble might be replaced by the ugly might. The future of humanity lies in our trust in God and our belief that this world is the best possible world that we could have inherited from our ancestors. Let us believe that we should not destroy it for the sake of those who will come after us, because God only knows the ends of all things and the beginnings of all springs.

All of us should stand firm in the belief that we know neither the beginning nor the end of the world. Ours is the middle of the road from the eternity *(ezel)* that is out of our touch and to the eternity *(ebed)* that is out of our reach. By the mercy of our Lord, we are not left alone in the middle of our journey from the eternity to the eternity—we have the Word of God that was in the beginning and that will be in the end. We claim that we are committed to strive for hope, love, and justice. But whose hope, whose love, and whose justice? Don't we realize that love and justice must temper the Jewish hope? Don't we, equally, see that hope and justice must follow the Christian love for a neighbor? And finally, don't we agree that hope and love must come out with the Muslim justice for all?

It is in the context of the Muslim commitment to justice for all that I would like to offer you two doctrinal and historical Islamic principles that everyone can share. First, it is the clear statement of the Holy Qur'an, "la ikraha fil-din," "Let there be no compulsion in religion,"[13] a statement that brought the idea of freedom of religion, or freedom of conscience, that is considered today to be one of the most fundamental values of our globe. Should I remind you that as recently as September 27, 1480, the Spanish sovereigns Ferdinand and Isabella issued an order to establish in their kingdoms tribunals to judge cases of "heretical depravity," to become known as the Spanish Inquisition. This fact of history Professor Benzion Netanyahu brings to our attention in this way: "The royal decree explicitly stated that the Inquisition was instituted to search out and punish converts from Judaism who transgressed against Christianity by secretly adhering to Jewish beliefs and performing rites and ceremonies of the Jews."[14]

My intention here is not to embarrass any person or religion, but to show the significance of the testimony of Stanford Shaw, the Jewish author, who has this to say about an interesting political as well as moral legacy of Islam:

> Neither the people of the Republic of Turkey nor those of Europe and America fully realize the extent to which Turkey, and the Ottoman Empire which preceded it, over the centuries served as major places of refuge for people suffering from persecution, Muslims and non-Muslims alike, from the fourteenth century to the present. In many ways, the Turks historically fulfilled the role subsequently taken up by the United States of America beginning in the late nineteenth century.[15]

I have quoted this witness not because I think that one can justify all the historical actions of the Ottoman sultans, but to demonstrate that it was due to the above-mentioned short but very powerful Qur'anic statement of the seventh century that the Muslim scholars developed the concept of the protection of five fundamental rights, what we call today "human rights," of each and every person regardless of his or her religion or nationality: the right to life (*nafs*), the right to religion (*din*), the right to freedom ('*aql*), the right to property (*mal*), and the right to dignity ('*ird*).

It is quite regrettable that the modern Muslim intelligentsia has failed to pick up on this doctrinal and historical foundation of an Islamic avant-garde for human rights to build up social, political, and moral institutions in the Muslim world that would guarantee the development of a genuine democratic system. What more is needed for the modern Muslim intelligentsia to know about the intellectual legacy of Islam after the testimony of the prominent historian Arnold Toynbee (1889–1975), who wrote concerning the work of the great Muslim intellectual Ibn Khaldun (1332–1406): "He conceived and formulated a philosophy of history which is undoubtedly the greatest work of its kind that has ever yet been produced by any mind in any time or place."[16] There is nothing to be added to this testimony, except to affirm that the failure to advance culture further lies not in Islam, but in the cultural insecurity of the modern Muslim intelligentsia that has failed to collect the delicious intellectual fruits, such as that of Ibn Khaldul and many other Muslim intellectuals.

One of the reasons that I am here in full capacity as a Muslim of the European origin is the universal declaration of equal rights that the Prophet Muhammad (peace be upon him) had delivered at one of his ceremonies on the hill of Arafat when he said: "Kullukum min adam wa'adam min turab, la fadl li'arabi 'ala 'ajami, wala li'ajami 'ala 'arabi, wala li'abyad 'ala aswad, wala li'aswad 'ala abyad illa bitaqwa." ("You are all children of Adam, and Adam is from clay. Let there be no superiority of an Arab over a non-Arab, nor a non-Arab over an Arab, and neither shall be a superiority of a white over a black, nor a black over a white person, except by good character.")[17]

I don't know whether the American Baptist minister and leader of the civil rights movement from 1963, the most honorable Martin

Luther King Jr., was aware of the above-mentioned universal declaration of the Prophet Muhammad (peace be upon him), but I do
know that we are all in a desperate need today to listen to those
divinely inspired messages. Of course, I am aware that my power is
too frail to be King's voice, but my heart is full of hope to have Martin Luther King's dreams today as his were yesterday that my three
children will one day live in a world where they will not be judged
by the faith of their heart but by the content of their character. And,
I am equally enthusiastic to tell you that I believe in Martin Luther
King's insight that "the choice today is not between violence or nonviolence; it is either nonviolence or nonexistence."

We should have understood by now that no one has the monopoly on righteousness, no one has the monopoly on retaliation, and
no one has the monopoly on pain. On the contrary, we are all entitled to do right things and to be recognized thereby. We are all
designated to strive and protect our freedoms, and we are all vulnerable to the pain, whether it comes from the democratically elected
government or from voluntary suicidal individuals or groups.

In light of these thoughts I invite you to have hope, love, and justice for all that Jews, Christians, and Muslims can deliver to the world,
which needs to be freed from fear and poverty now more than ever
before, and I call you to join me in a Bosnian prayer:

Our Lord
Do not let success deceive us
Nor failure take us to despair!
Always remind us that failure is a temptation
That precedes success!
Our Lord
Teach us that tolerance is the highest degree of power
And the desire for revenge
The first sign of weakness!
Our Lord
If you deprive us of our property,
Give us hope!
If you grant us with success,
Give us also the will to overcome defeat!
If you take from us the blessings of health,
Provide us with the blessing of faith!

Our Lord
If we sin against people,
Give us the strength of apology
And if people sin against us,
Give us the strength of forgiveness!
Our Lord
If we forget Thee,
Do not forget us!

NOTES

1. Alija Izetbegovic, "Mir je spasio Bosnu (Peace Saved Bosnia)," in *Godisnjak 2002 BZK Preporod*, Sarajevo, 2002, 20.

2. Alija Izetbegovic, *Notes from Prison, 1983–1988* (Westport, Conn.: Praeger, 2002); *Inescapable Questions (Autobiographic Notes)* (Leicester: The Islamic Foundation, 2003).

3. "The Sabians seem to have been a monotheistic religious group intermediate between Judaism and Christianity." See *The Message of the Qur'an,* translated and explained by Muhammad Asad (Gibraltar: Dar al-Andalus, 1984), 14 n 49.

4. Stephen Schwartz, *The Two Faces of Islam* (New York: Doubleday, 2002), 2.

5. "The New Testament by John," in the *Holy Bible, New International Version* (Zondervan, 1993), 505.

6. "About what do they (most often) ask one another? About the great word (*al-Nabe'u-l-azim*) on which they disagree. Nay, but at the end they will come to understand it" (Qur'an, 78:1–4).

7. 'Imad el-Din ibn Kathir al-Qurashi al-Dimashqi, *el-Bidajetu we el-Nihajetu,* uredio 'Abdullah el-Turki (Dar el-Hidzrah, 1996).

8. Dom Aelred Graham, *The End of Religion* (New York: Harcourt Brace Jovanovich, 1971).

9. John Horgan, *The End of Science* (London: Abacus, 1998).

10. Ibid., 23–24.

11. Francis Fukuyama, *The End of History and the Last Man* (New York: Free Press, 1992).

12. John Lukacs, *At the End of an Age* (New Haven: Yale University Press, 2002).

13. See *The Holy Qur'an,* translation and commentary by A. Yusif Ali (Lahore, 1934), 103.

14. See B. Netanyahu, *The Origins of the Inquisition in Fifteenth-Century Spain* (New York: Random House, 1995), 3.

15. See Standford J. Shaw, *Turkey and the Holocaust* (London: Ipswich Books, 1993), 1.

16. See Arnold Toynbee, *A Study of History* (London: Oxford University Press, 1934), vol. 3, 322.

17. See A. J. Wensinck and J. P. Mensing, *Concordance et Indicies de la Tradition Musulmane* (Leiden, 1969), vol. 7, 300.

3

God Is the All-Peace, the All-Merciful

Mohamed Fathi Osman

From the Qur'an:

God is the All-Peace Who Calls Humankind to Peace

"He is the All-Merciful, the Mercy-giving. God is He save whom there is no deity; the Sovereign Supreme, the Holy, the All-Peace" (Qur'an 59:22–23).

"And God calls [the human beings] into the abode of peace, and guides one who wills onto a straight way. Those who persevere in doing good, they will get the ultimate good" (10:25–26).

"O you who have attained to faith! Enter all wholly into peace, and follow not Satan's footsteps, for, verily, he is your open foe" (2:208).

Condemning destruction of life

"And among the humankind there is the one whose views on this world life would please you, and would cite God as witness to what is in his [/her] heart, and he [/she] is the most contentious of adversaries in dispute. As this one gets away, he [/she] goes about the earth spreading damage and destroying tilth and progeny; and God does not love causing damage. And whenever he [/she] is told, 'Be conscious of God,' he [/she] adds arrogance to guilt; and for him [/her] hell will be well-deserved, and how vile a resting place!" (2:204–6).

"Even if you draw forth your hand toward me to kill me, I shall never draw forth my hand toward you to kill you; I fear God, the Lord of the whole universe. Let you bear my wrongdoings as well as yours, and then you would be destined for fire and that is the requital of evildoers" (5:28–29).

"In consequence, We did ordain unto the children of Israel [and all believers who follow] that if anyone kills a human being—unless it be [in punishment] for murder or for spreading damage on earth— it shall be as though he had killed all humankind: whereas, if any- one saves a human life, it shall be as though he had saved the lives of all humankind" (5:32).

Repelling evil with good

"And a requital for a wrongdoing is equal to it, but whoever for- gives and makes peace [with the other], his [/her] reward rests with God; He, verily, does not love the transgressors" (42:40).

"But for any who defends himself [/herself] after having suffered injustice, no blame attaches to them; blame attaches but to those who are guilty of wrongdoing against [other] people and commit aggression on earth against all right . . . but withal, if one is patient in adversity and forgives, this is what ought to be determined" (42:41–43).

"And if you have to respond to an attack, respond only to the extent of the attack leveled against you; but to bear yourselves with patience is indeed far better for those who are patient in adversity" (16:126).

"And it may well be that God will bring about affection between you and those whom you are facing now as enemies, and God is All- Powerful, and God is Much-Forgiving, Mercy-Giving" (60:7).

"But good and evil cannot be equal, repel you [evil] with what is better, and so the one between whom and yourself was enmity, [may then become] as though he [/she] would be a close friend. Yet this is not given to any but those endowed with great destiny" (4:34–35).

Resources for nonviolence are at the center of Islam

The above-mentioned verses of the Qur'an, God's revealed Book to Prophet Muhammad, indicate essential Islamic precepts that provide a solid foundation for going beyond violence. God is the All-Peace who calls on the whole humankind in general and the Muslims in particular to enter all wholly into peace. The Creator of life sharply condemns aggression and destroying life, whatever the delusive argument and rhetoric supporting such actions may be. Further, the Qur'an urges to repel the wrongdoing with self-control and reconciliation, for this is much rewarded in this world in dealing with the wrongdoer, who may be turned one day into a friend, and it is highly rewarded in the eternal life to come. Patience and self-control are stressed in the Qur'an more than eighty-five times; forgiveness, not only patience, is stressed more than twenty times. In addition, there are basic doctrinal and moral principles that establish going beyond violence in the deepest depth of the Muslim minds and hearts.

A basic meeting point for all the believers in the One God, including Muslims, is that He is the Creator of life and the Lord of all human beings, and the entire creation. Accordingly, a strong, rational, and hearty relationship is felt by the human being toward all humans, the whole life, and the entire cosmos. Consequently, such a believer should never be the one who acts violently toward any of the marvels of God's creation, and humans stand in the front. All humans are equal creations of God and enjoy life given to them by God, and the true believer in the Lord's creation should extol God's limitless glory in securing and preserving His wonders of creation. Committing any aggression against any of these wonders is simply an attack against the believer's faith and sensibility. The true faith in the All-Peace, the All-Merciful has to radiate peace within the human self, and through the relations with all human beings and all creation. God with all His attributes, and in the Creator-creation relationship in the Abrahamic monotheism, is distinguished from god in superstition, philosophy, science, and even passive mysticism. Filled with peace from the All-Peace, the believer should not be shaken by enormous power or weakness, arrogance, or despair. The believer always enjoys a state of balance and peacefulness from within, which is reflected in all his/her relations with others, human or living or being. How can the believer violate the equal rights of equal humans in enjoying peace within himself and with others, the invaluable blessing of the faith in the All-Peace?

A spirit from God is in every human being

God confers dignity on all humans, and the human mind is God's invaluable gift for human conception and interaction whatever one's ethnicity, gender, belief, or opinion may be. The Qur'an states that God mentioned to the angels about the creation of the human being: "And when I have fully formed him and breathed into him of my spirit, fall down before him in prostration" (15:29, 38:72). The Qur'an clearly indicates that this spirit from God is in all children of Adam, and in their successive generations, "and whenever your Lord brings forth from the loins of the children of Adam their offspring, He [thus] calls upon them to bear witness about themselves: 'Am I not your Lord?' And to that they say, 'Yes, indeed, we bear witness thereto!'" (7:172). Accordingly, every human being is a potential believer, as well as being favored by dignity from God as a human being: "We have conferred dignity on the children of Adam, and have borne them over land and sea, and have provided for them sustenance out of the good things of life, and have favored them far above most of Our creation" (17:70).

Besides this spiritual compass, the human mind is a common human merit granted by the Creator, so the whole humankind should communicate together through these divine blessings using reason and common sense. The Qur'an addresses and motivates the human senses and sensibility in about a hundred verses. Violence is a rebellious denial of God's blessings and human virtues as well. In the Islamic terminology, "the good," or virtue, is called "the well-recognized by all *'al-ma'ruf'* " and "the bad," or evil, is called "the well-rejected by all *'al-munkar.'* "

Human diversity

Human diversity, which can never be ignored or stopped, should not provoke hostility nor obstruct reasonable communication among human beings; on the contrary it enriches human experience and allows a complementation of different human views and efforts. Human diversity is one of God's wonders in His creation (30:22), and it is meant to let humankind know one another and complement one another through a universal intellectual and practical cooperation: "and We have made you into nations and tribes so that you might come to know one another" (49:13).

People naturally have their inborn or acquired differences, but they can argue fruitfully and ethically together and reach common ground: "And had your Lord so willed, He could surely have made all humankind one single community, but [He willed it otherwise, and so] they continue to have divergence, [all of them] save these upon whom your Lord has bestowed His grace [by following God's guidance in handling the differences conceptually and ethically], and to this end [of testing human beings through handling their differences] He has created them [all]" (11:118–19).

Even with regard to religion, the Qur'an teaches that human diversity also applies: "Unto every [community] of you [humans] have We appointed a [different] law and practical way of behavior; and if God had so willed, He could surely have made you all one single community, but [He willed it otherwise] so as to test you through what He has given unto you. Vie, then, with one another in doing good works. Unto God you all must return, and then He will make you truly understand all that on which you were used to differ" (5:48; see also 2:148). That the judgment of one's faith has to be left to God on the Day of Judgment is repeatedly emphasized in various phrasing, about twenty-five times in the Qur'an. Conceptual and ethical guidance in argument is indicated in numerous Qur'anic verses through the entire Book (e.g., 4:59; 6:152; 7:148; 16:125; 17:53; 23:96; 29:46; 39:18; 41:34; 49:6, 11–12). The Qur'an stresses the principle of "conversation in the most proper and constructive way [al-jidaf-bi-allati hiya ahsan]" between different parties: within the family, the community, and all different communities and groups (e.g., 2:233; 16:125; 29:46).

"No coercion is ever allowed in matters of faith" (2:251)

Naturally, the only way for a faith is through voluntary conviction and acceptance. Accordingly, any use of force to impose whatever is related to the faith is meaningless and contradicts the psychological and the religious principles. The Qur'an sharply prohibits any coercion in matters of faith (2:251). Further, the Qur'an reads, "And had your Lord so willed, all those who live on earth would surely have attained to faith, all of them; do you then think that you could compel people to believe?" (10:99). This has been repeatedly emphasized through the Qur'an (e.g., 10:99; 11:28; 22:87–88; 50:45). Whoever thinks that violence can be a way to establish the faith is not really aware of the nature of each, and how contradictory both are.

Favorable moral climate, cooperation, and competition in good doing with all humans under peace

If hostility and violence have to be avoided, the minds and hearts would be open for more friendly and constructive relations. Good feelings, justice, and care ought to be nurtured in Muslims' relations with others (e.g., 60:7–8); and meeting the other's feelings, thoughts, or actions, even if they are not good, with "that is better, magnanimous, and more rewarding," in this world life and in the eternal life to come, is an expression that is stressed many times in the Qur'an. The believer is urged to understand patience not as a mechanical practice, but to make one's patience untainted, wholesome, virtuous, and in one word "beautiful," as the Quran describes it (2:18, 83; 70:5); and the same is required in case of forgiveness (15:85), and even in case of dissociation from a person or group (33:28, 49; 73:10). Justice has to be conducted in the best and most effective and noblest way, and going beyond justice to what is better and more rewarding in human relations and in God's valuation is underscored throughout the Qur'an (e.g., 2:178, 229, 231, 237, 280). Universal cooperation in doing good is urged (5:2; 60:7–8). Further, constructive competition within the diverse humanity is urged in the Qur'an: "And every community has its direction of which He lets them turn towards it. Vie, therefore, with one another in doing good works. Wherever you may be, God will gather you all unto Him" (2:148). "Unto every one of you have We appointed a [different] law and practical way of behavior . . . Vie, then, with one another in doing good works. Unto God you all must return" (5:48).

Muslims should never initiate war, and in self-defense they have to return to peace whenever it is offered

War is not allowed by the Islamic law *Shari'a* and was never practiced in the time of the Prophet except for self-defense against aggression (22:39–40; 4:75). Legal and ethical principles in confronting the enemy in the battlefield pave the way for restoring peace, by trying to reduce the bitterness of the hostility through restricting military operations to the combatants only, honoring any promise or agreement, and caring about the wounded and the prisoners of war. Meanwhile, any attitude toward peace from the aggressors has to be seriously considered, whatever doubts about their intentions may be: "And if they incline to peace, incline you to peace and place your trust in God; verily, He alone is All-Hearing, All-Knowing. And should they seek to deceive you, behold, God is enough [security] for you" (8:61–62). Any agreement should be based on justice, not on military prevalence: "And if they revert, make peace with them according to justice, and deal equitably with them, for verily, God loves those who act equitably" (49:9). Agreements with any parts during peace or after war should be observed and carried out honestly, and any breach of an agreement, even if it was through word of mouth, is a deadly sin (e.g., 5:1; 13:20; 16:91–95; 17:34; 23:8, 70:32).

Resources Have Not Been Well Functioning among Adherents: Malpractice and Misconceptions of *Jihad*

In the time of the Prophet Muhammad (d. 11H./632), war was only an answer to an attack and its only purpose was self-defense. Under the early two caliphs Abu Bakr (11–13H./632–34) and Umar (13–23H./634–44), securing the borders of the Arabian peninsula, which had entirely become a Muslim land, was not left to go smoothly from the two great near eastern powers in the middle ages: the Byzantine and the Sasanian empires, which neighbored Arabia from the north and the east, respectively. Early worry about the emerging message and authority in Arabia had been signaled by each in the time of the Prophet, but the actual engagement with their extensive well-trained and well-equipped armies occurred under the early two caliphs, who were both unwilling and unprepared for it.

However, it may be said that the expansion for the sake of expansion took place later. The Umayyads who reached power in the Muslim state by force, not through a free public choice as before, established a hereditary dynasty and ruled harshly, tried—as all despots—to turn the attention of their oppressed people to external fronts and victorious expansion. Under the founder of the Umayyad dynasty

Mu'awiya (40–60H./660–80), conquests in Asia eastward of the Sasanian lands continued, as well as in North Africa, and Constantinople, which was besieged by land and sea under the leadership of the crown prince Yazid in the year 48H./668. Under al-Walid ibn Abd al-Malik (86–96H./705–15), conquests of Transoxiana, northern India, and southern Spain (al-Andalus) went on. Alongside with such Umayyad expansion, civil wars, rebellions, and oppressions never ceased: al-Husayn, the grandson of the Prophet, and another descendant of the Prophet were killed; and ironically, as Constantinople witnessed an Umayyad siege that failed, Mecca and Medina, the two sacred cities in Islam, were also besieged by the Umayyad armies in 61H./680 and 73H./692 because of their rebellions against the Umayyads, which were fiercely crushed.

When the Umayyad dynasty fell as a result of its internal cracks and the finishing stroke of the Abbasids, their successors followed the same policy of internal suppression and external wars. It was reported that the distinguished Abbasid caliph al-Rashid (170–193H./786–809) used to go regularly to Mecca for a pilgrimage one year and for conquest the next year, and he had a headdress on which his characteristics "conqueror-pilgrim" were embroidered! Such an expansionist trend continued through successive dynasties; it extended and even grew among the converted peoples to Islam, tempted by the circumstantial and communal admiration of conquests and conquerors in the name of Islam.

The distinguished jurist Sufyan al-Thawri (d. 161H./778) in Iraq was among those who persistently emphasized that jihad is a religious duty only in the case of defense. However, others like al-Awza'i (d. 157H./774) in Syria, Abu Hanifa (d. 150H/767) in Iraq, and a pillar of the Hanafi school Muhammad ibn al-Hasan al-Shaybani (d. 189H/804) represented the expansionist trend and held that war is legitimate to spread the message of Islam in a land where its authorities do not accept voluntarily the faith or the payment of a tribute jizya. The obligation for such a war is collective and considered according to the ability to fulfill its fard kifaya. The whole Muslim community, umma, is held responsible for this obligation and whenever any part of it is able to fulfill it, this would be a fulfillment for the entire community, which is different from responding to an attack on the Muslims, when every Muslim individual is held responsible for defending the attacked people and land *(fard'ayn)*. Since the Byzantines turned to attack the Muslim lands instead of receiving the Muslim attacks, the trend for aggressive war increased and prevailed, especially when it was supported by the distinguished jurist al-Shafi'i (d. 204H./820). The distinguished jurist Malik ibn Anas (d. 179H./795) in Medina seemed, through his answers to questions about jihad under the Umayyads, not wholeheartedly supportive, but merely not objecting in light of the detrimental development against the Muslims at the Byzantine borders.[1]

Islamic jurisprudence on jihad grew up under a climate of expansion and carried on such a trend through different periods and rulers. The Ottoman sultans were keen and proud to have the title *ghazi* ("conqueror"), and even "Kemal Ataturk" (d. 1938), the founder and the first president of modern secular Republic of Turkey in 1922, was sometimes called *ghazi* when he confronted successfully the European occupiers of Turkey after the Ottoman defeat in World War I (1914–18). Even in late centuries of weakness, jurists just maintained and repeated the views of earlier leading imams, since the practice of *ijtihad,* the intellectual effort for reaching new rulings according to the developing circumstances, had already stopped. This visionless repetition of what had been compiled before simply echoed the view of a continuous war for spreading Islam all over the world, which might be merely a consolation for Muslims in these times of weakness. Under European colonization, jihad was reviewed and raised as a banner of resistance and struggle.

THE IMPACT OF COLONIZATION:
POLARIZATION OF *SALAFISM* AND MODERNISM

Through the confrontation with European colonialism, the hostile and aggressive trend among Muslims against "the others," now the advanced European colonists, was nurtured. Oversimplifying the problems, Muslims in modern times thought that sticking to the juristic heritage regarding power—not moral power, which is the essence of faith in God and is always supportive and productive, but physical power—and about universal confrontation would let them pass the present with all its weakness and humiliation and restore the past with all its glories.

Some Muslims, however, have thought that the power in modern times belongs to Europe and that they have to follow its model in order to gain power. This attitude failed to preserve the authentic roots in their pure essence, maintaining the positiveness of their heritage and building on such solid grounds what may be positive in modern times. A polarization has occurred between advocates of the historical model of power in the Muslim heritage, which may be called the "Salafism" in its narrowest representation, or misrepresentation, and the modern model of power in Europe, which may be called "modernism," whose advocates might not be less extreme than the Salafis. Selective extracts from the Muslim heritage or from the European modern thought and practices, especially from the views of some antireligion or anti-Islam thinkers, have made the polarization unsurpassable. Later Muslim apologetics could not attract many in both parties.

Secularism of the modern state could not be objectively understood nor fairly judged by the advocates of the heritage, who have restricted themselves to the model of the Muslim past, or even the model of the early Muslim past. They have failed to perceive any positive or constructive element in a secular state, or even any acceptable definition of the word, which may have various definitions in different times and places. The Muslim historical civilization as it was known in Damascus, Baghdad, Cairo, Fez, and Cordova, which might be close to the essence of being called secular in a sense, has been rejected by the Salafis as un-Islamic or at least non-Islamic, while it has been completely disregarded by the wholesale advocates of modernity, including secularism.

The Salafi trend, with a connection to jihad among some groups, has used the negatives of the postcolonial national governments, whether they have a democratic pretense or autocratic nature, to attack modernism, which could not be judged for many Muslims separately from Europe and the West in general. These governments often have been supported by one Western power or another, however oppressive and corrupted they may have been. Further, the Western attitude toward political and economical domination supported by technological and military superiority has added to the ammunition of the supporters of Salafism against modernism, especially the proponents of jihad, which has become directed against both the Western powers and their internal allies. Recently we have experienced in the American-British war in Iraq an example of issued religious rulings *(fatawa)* from the Iraqi opposition side against Saddam Husayn (Hussein), or from the opponents of the American-British attack against it. Such a climate has allowed the juristic heritage of jihad and militancy to be strongly revived, with inevitable tones and actions of violence.

PROBLEMS IN DEALING WITH THE SACRED SOURCES

As Salafism (and militancy) has found a favorable climate in the external and internal circumstances of the Muslim peoples, it has been affected by certain problems in dealing with the sacred sources. No distinction has been in general realized between the permanent divine sources and the human elaborations on and derivations from these, which have been inevitably influenced by the changing circumstances of time and place, including the sociocultural situation of the community and the author. There is also no comprehensive pursuit of the difference in views on a certain issue through different times and places, or on the causes of differences or the reasoning for each view, although the divine sources are always the same. Such a tracing, if it happens, could clarify and stress the human side of religious thought and the changeability, dynamism, and limitations, at the same time, of this human product. The Qur'an and the Prophet's traditions (Sunna) came out through the whole message of Islam, which took twenty-three years, and these traditions have to be considered in their development and entirely, not in detachment or in part.

According to certain structural and circumstantial indicators, the command has various grades of obligation, encouragement, or mere guidance, and the interdiction has various grades of prohibition or discouragement. Everything is in principle allowed unless it is proven rightfully to be interdicted. In discussing an issue, the goals and general principles of the Islamic law, *Shari'a,* should be considered differently from the dominant approach of splitting and isolating certain texts. With regard to the Sunna, some traditions might present the Prophet's view according to this human experience, as an individual or as a leader of his community in its given circumstances. In both cases, such a view cannot be considered a permanent legal rule.[2]

Further, the Qur'an and the Sunna addressed directly the actual Arabian situation to reform it, just as they address the Muslims and all humanity in every time and place. If the message of Islam should care only about the general, it would never attract or convince the Arabs in the seventh century, and accordingly could never reach others in different times and places. On the other hand, if it addressed only the particular Arab situation in the time of the message, it would never find an acceptance among other peoples in different circumstances. The sacred sources have addressed the particular and the universal concerns side by side, sometimes explicitly and in most times implicitly. One has to find out the structural and historical indicators to make a distinction between the permanent universal and the transient particular. Such research considers the circumstances in which the particular Qur'anic verse or the Prophet's tradition came out, as well as the sociocultural history of Arabia before Islam and in the time of the message in general. Many verses in the Qur'an may be merely historical, reporting certain events, which happened in the time of the Prophet, from which people in any time get a moral message, not a legal rule. The Qur'an includes more than 375 verses related to jihad, within 6,246 verses in the entire Book related to the faith, moral values, previous prophets and their messages, acts of worship, and laws in their various areas. Among these more than 375 Qur'anic verses related to jihad and the battles of the early Muslims, only about 61 verses present permanent legal rules about war, its legitimate reasons, practice, consequences, and so on.

In addition, in every religion, you see statements with an inclusive character, alongside others, which seem exclusive. Together they make a right equation, and both have to be taken in perspective. The Qur'an addresses sometimes the "children of Adam," sometimes "the people," and sometimes "the individual human being," and it also addresses "the believers." Each address has its significance and indication.

THE IMPACT OF PRESENT SOCIOCULTURAL FACTORS

Contemporary Muslims, then, face formidable challenges with regard to the impact of colonialism followed by postcolonial domination of the West, the polarization and conflict of Salafism and modernism, and the problems of dealing with their religious heritage.

They have been facing such an appallingly complex defiance, while they have been suffering from the huge burden of successive centuries of political powerlessness, socioeconomic lag, and cultural impotence. Illiteracy has been dominant, and the absence of freedom of opinion, expression, and association have been crippling the educated small minority from a serious and fruitful tackling of challenges, interacting with the masses, and developing the simple vague aspirations into a serious intellectual and social progressive movement. Such a climate enhances hostilities within the Muslims and with others, and is most likely favorable for thinking about violence and practicing it.

The ideas about the universal struggle of the oppressed and mass revolutions, especially the Marxist-Leninist ideology, supported by technological development in producing the means of violence at reasonable costs, have provided the discontented with ideological and practical tools, which they easily "Islamized," by building on the partial selective understanding of jihad in the heritage of the past, without making any distinction between the interim particular and the permanent universal, nor between the differences in the given circumstances of time and place. The technological development of oppressive measures and war weapons on the side of the state has made such conflicts with such violent militants dreadful on both sides, for both suffer in the final account, and those who suffer most are the public majority and humanity, and above all the message of God, the All-Peace, the All-Merciful, which is erroneously thought to be best served with what contradicts its essence: hostility, violence, and bloodshed.

In the Ten Commandments we find "Thou shall not kill" (Exodus 20:13); in the Gospel according to St. Matthew, Jesus said to the one who drew out his sword against those who came to seize him, "Put up again thy sword into his place; for all they that take the sword shall perish with the sword" (Matthew 26:52). The Qur'an states: "And [an attempt at] requiting evil may, too, become an evil; hence, whoever pardons and makes peace, his reward rests with God; for, verily, He does not love evildoers" (42:40). On this verse, the late European thinker Muhammad Asad (d. 1992) commented: "In other words, successful struggle against tyranny [which is mentioned in the previous verse (*baghy,* in Arabic) as a reason for confrontation] often tends to degenerate into a similarly tyrannical attitude toward the erstwhile oppressors."[3]

Gilles Kepel wrote in the *Time* special issue of "9/11 One Year Later" under the title "Will the Jihad Ever Catch Fire?"

> The extremist supporters of the U.S. attacks have posted a disastrous record during the past year. In their principal objective—to mobilize the Muslim masses behind a victorious jihad that would overthrow existing regimes and replace them with Islamic states—the extremists have failed utterly. . . . The attacks had only limited consequences and did not destabilize pro-Western regimes to any degree or permit radicals to seize power . . . [As for directing the jihadists' violence towards Israel,] suicide attacks have proved so repugnant in Europe and the U.S. that they have begun to erode support for the Palestinian cause there. They have contributed significantly to the free hand wielded by Israeli Prime Minister Ariel Sharon, who has completely destroyed the infrastructure of the West Bank. Palestinian intellectuals and members of civil society have also recognized the bombings as a political disaster and are leading calls for their immediate halt. . . . The price will eventually undermine the reputation and allure of the most radical Palestinian militants, as it did in the 1990s, when terror strategies were curtailed in Egypt and Algeria. The question is how many innocents will die before the zealots move on.[4]

On the other hand, meeting violence from below by violence from above has crystallized in all minds the wisdom and foresight of Jesus' words, "All they that take the sword shall perish with the sword." The Russian president Vladimir Putin, former KGB man,

> is already using [the] resurgent nationalism to build support for a new offensive in Chechnya . . . but Putin's war is going nowhere. Russian soldiers in Chechnya have killed more than 13,000 Chechen rebels since 1999, but the brutality of the army's tactics has spawned new, more fanatical fighters faster than it has eliminated the old ones. Before the hostage siege [at the Moscow theater], 57% of the public supported talks with the rebels; last week that number had slipped, but not by much, to 44% . . . Russians are still waiting for Putin to prove he can deliver more than tough talks.[5]

It is the responsibility of believers in God to rethink over and over how by all means can such a fierce attitude toward violence from below and from above be turned toward "beyond violence" in solving deeply rooted psychological-mental complexes, as well as emerging problems. Secularism means the separation of state from any religion in its particularities and clerical institutions, not from the universal moral principles, on the top of which is the sanctity of human life. The concepts of "self-defense," "just war," and "jihad" have to be reviewed in the light of modern technological development and the horrible destructive products it provides for terrorist groups and government military forces as well. The efforts and costs of violence would be better rewarded if such efforts were directed to support democracy and social-cultural development in Muslim countries through productive and peaceful means and to strengthen the United Nations and its bodies in settling disputes about human rights within the Muslim countries, or in the relations between Muslim countries or between them and others, in addition to assisting the development in all developing countries.

Schools and the media have an essential role to nurture a trend of common moral peaceful responsibility, which replaces the dominant exaggerated individualist and materialist tendency under a climate of egocentrism within the individual, the community, or the nation. Nothing like the call of God the All-Peace, the All-Merciful, can heal the wounds in the deepest depths of the human hearts and minds and over the various areas of human activities. Specialists in all areas have to be involved. Those who are sincere and serious in going "beyond violence" have to act soon, in a united front, for this challenge is grave, and such a stand, if it is made without delay, may be a turning point in the cultural history of the world, and hopefully in the political and military history also.

We have to rush to the rescue of the mounting numbers of victims of frustration and lack of depth in our current life in spite of amazing material achievements. John Walker Lindh, the bright young boy from suburban America, ended up alongside the Taliban in Afghanistan, and numerous Muslim boys have been similarly going through "a story of love, loathing and an often reckless quest for spiritual fulfillment . . . [they] went off to find purity and peace, and found fanaticism and war," as John's story has been put in *Time*.[6]

Sana Shah is a young victim of the violence from above.

She has been to the U.S. and has an expansive, tolerant outlook on global affairs . . . her mother is the daughter of a famous army general, her father an economist . . . after September 11 she felt caught between the two worlds she loves. Rising Islamic militancy in Pakistan made her question the roots of her faith, but America's military response to the New York City and Washington attacks made her profoundly disillusioned . . . she felt revulsion at the U.S. air strikes, which left hundreds of Afghans dead and thousands more wounded . . ." Why is an Afghan's life worth any less than an American's?" she asks. . . . Suddenly to Sana, America went from being the "next best thing to home," as her mother put it, to being an arrogant bully . . . Sana's parents are tolerant but pious, and their example helped her resist the radicals' taunts at Lahore Grammar School . . . Sana still feels trapped between worlds . . . She is still a moderate citizen of the world and still believes in peace.[7]

Shouldn't we mobilize all believers in God and in peace, and sharpen our minds and wills, to keep such invaluable assets of young men and women "beyond violence," beyond disillusion and confusion, and beyond frustration? Certainly we should, and we pray to the All-Peace, the All-Merciful, for guidance and strength.

NOTES

1. Muhammad ibn al-Hasan Al-Shaybani, *al-Siyar al-Kabir,* as dictated and commented on by Muhammad ibn Ahmad al-Sarakhsi, ed. Al-Munajjid, Salah al-Din, Ma'had al-Makhtutat al-Arabiyya (Cairo: League of Arab States, 1971), vol. 1, 187–91. See also Roy Parviz Mottahedeh and Ridwan al-Sayyid, "The Idea of the Jihad in Islam Before the Crusades," in *The Crusades from the Perspective of Byzantine and the Muslim World,* ed. E. Laiou Angeliki and Roy Parviz Mottahedeh (Washington, D.C.: Dumbarton Oaks Research Library and Collection, 2001), 23–27.

2. See any book on "'Usul al-Fiqh," for example, Khallaf, 'Abd al-Wahhab, 'Ilm 'Usul al-Fiqh, Dar al-Qalam (al-Kuwait, 1978), 43–44; also al-Qarafi, Ahmad ibn-Idris, al-Ihkam fi Tamyiz al-Fatawa'an al-'Ahkam wa Tasarrufat al-Qadi wa al-Iman, ed. Abu Ghudda, Abd al-Fattah, Maktab al-Matbu'at al-Islamiyyah (Aleppo, 1967), esp. 86–109.

3. Muhammad Asad, *The Message of the Quran* (Dar al-Andalus: Gilbralter, 1984), comment on verse 42:40, 746, n 40.

4. Gilles Kepel, "Will the Jihad Ever Catch Fire?" *Time,* Sept. 11, 2002, 94–95.

5. Romesh Ratnsear and Paul Quinn-Judge, "Russian to the Core," *Time,* Nov. 11, 2002, 56.

6. Timothy Roche et al., "The Making of John Walker Lindh," *Time,* Oct. 7, 2002, 44, 46.

7. Tim McGrik, "MTV or the Muezzin," *Time,* Sept. 11, 2002, 90–93.

Judaism on Violence and Reconciliation: An Examination of Key Sources

Reuven Firestone

Christians have sometimes claimed that Judaism is a violent religion and the God of Israel is a violent God. The accusation tends to be made in relation to Christianity as a religion of peace and the God of Christianity as expressing only love.[1] As a student of religion in general as well as Judaism in particular, I must admit that I know of no criteria through which one can judge a religion as violent or merciful, cruel or compassionate, just or perverse. Such judgments of religion tend to be made on the basis of only a few, carefully chosen scriptural sources.

Then again, some Jewish scriptural sources certainly seem incriminating. God is even named explicitly in the famous "Song of the Sea" as the God of war: "YHW[2] is a man of war; YHW is His name" (Ex. 15:3).[3]

Some scriptural texts boast that the Israelites destroyed every man, woman, and child of enemy communities that they encountered. In Deuteronomy 3:3–6, for example, we read: "So the Lord our God also delivered into our power King Og of Bashan, with all his men, and we dealt them such a blow that no survivor was left . . . we captured all his towns; there was not a town that we did not take from them: sixty towns. . . . We doomed them as we had done in the case of King Sihon of Heshbon; we doomed every town—men, women, and children—and retained as booty all the cattle and the spoil."

God himself is depicted in Deuteronomy as commanding the Israelites to commit genocide against the Canaanites (Deut.7: 1–2): "When Adonai your God brings you to the land that you are about to enter and possess, and He dislodges many nations before you— Hittites, Girgashites, Amorites . . . seven nations much larger than you—and Adonai your God delivers them to you and you defeat them, you must doom them to total destruction; grant them no terms and show then no mercy."

These difficult verses have been explained in a variety of ways to lessen their horror. Some attempts to make sense of them are nothing more than apologetics. Some explanations, however, have real substance. Perhaps the most revealing is the very act of placing the text in its rhetorical context. Take this citation about genocide against the Canaanites, for example. A famous rabbinic admonition is said to have been uttered by a Talmudic sage in a different context when engaged in an argument over the meaning of a biblical text. The sage, a woman named Beruria, is cited as saying "Shatya! Shefeyl leseyfa!" which means, "Fool, read to the end of the passage!" (Berakhot 10a). In the Deuteronomy passage just cited, the very next verse after our command to annihilate the Canaanites reads: ". . . and don't marry them!" If God's command had been annihilation there would have been no reason for the admonition not to intermarry with them, an observation that seems to fit what we know of the historical context of Deuteronomy. In seventh century B.C.E. Judah, where this text most likely emerged, Israelite religious culture was seriously threatened by the cultural and material superiority of the Canaanites. Rhetorically, therefore, the text at hand seems to read back into an earlier period of history, some five or six centuries before, when Israel was understood to have engaged in a "conquest" of the Land of Canaan.[4] The message therefore seems to have been that since Israel *should* have annihilated its Canaanite enemies but did not, it should most certainly not intermarry with them.

Contextualization is complex and is not always accurate. Indeed, it can be quite confusing and there remains disagreement among biblical scholars over the context of Deuteronomy. But as a colleague of mine is fond of saying, "My job is to complexify the situation!" First we shall complexify a bit. Then, I hope, we shall clarify.

Most readers do not resonate with these difficult verses. Another set of biblical messages is generally cited and preferred by biblicists, and clearly, verses teaching peace and reconciliation are also a part of the biblical tradition. Psalm 34, for example, which is recited in daily Jewish prayers, teaches a radically different approach from what we have just heard. The Psalmist writes: "Come, my children, listen to me; I will teach you what it is to be in awe of the Lord. Who is one who lusts for life, who desires (long) years of good fortune? Guard your tongue from evil, your lips from deceitful speech. Shun evil and do good. Seek shalom and pursue it" (Ps. 34:12–15).

This is indeed a lovely verse. It should be noted here that biblical scholars and linguists of ancient Hebrew generally do not consider the word *shalom* in this context to mean peace as cessation from war. They tend to use a word such as *amity* or *friendship*.[5] This verse may have intended to teach that reconciliation is one of the highest expressions of love for God.

Somewhat different, the famous verses from Isaiah 11 express deep longing for a safe world: "The wolf shall dwell with the lamb, the leopard lie down with the kid. The calf, the beast of prey shall feed together, with a little boy to herd them. The cow and the bear shall graze, their young shall lie down together; and the lion, like the ox, shall eat straw. A babe shall play over a viper's hole, and an infant pass his hand over an adder's den. In all of My sacred mount nothing evil or vile shall be done; for the earth shall be filled with devotion to the Lord as water covers the sea" (Isaiah 11:6–9).

But the method expressed in this passage for achieving safety might be objectionable. In this case we need to read the previous verse, which informs us of the means for achieving such safety: "[God] shall strike down the land with the rod of his mouth and slay the wicked with the breath of his lips." While it is true it is God and not humans who are engaging in the violence and killing, the passage is problematic from the perspectives of both ethics and theology.

Perhaps the most often-cited classic verses on reconciliation and peacemaking are the parallel statements in Isaiah and Micah that express longing for a future when all peoples will be unified under one God, and the nations "shall beat their swords into plowshares and their spears into pruning hooks; nation shall not take up sword against nation. They shall never again know war."[6] This message not only sounds like a wonderful poetic plea for a peaceful world, but it is said twice, suggesting its deep and lasting importance in the biblical worldview. But if we shift to the prophet Joel (4:9–10), we observe a different use of the same idiom: "Proclaim this among the nations: Prepare for battle! Arouse the warriors! Let all the fighters come and draw near! Beat your plowshares into swords, and your pruning hooks into spears."

It is extremely difficult in scriptural texts to separate metaphor from law and image from reality, and I should add here that this is a problem in every scripture of every religion. In the Hebrew Bible, it seems as if God represents peace and reconciliation one moment, while in the next, God represents violence and war. The Hebrew Bible may not be the best source for finding an unambiguous and commanding divine authority requiring acts of reconciliation and forbidding war as a means of response to conflict between peoples.

It would seem, therefore, that Judaism does not provide a positive role model for what we are seeking to accomplish in a conference the purpose of which is to move beyond violence. We might wish the Hebrew Bible to be consistent about peace and the elimination of violence, but we are confronted with the (sometimes) ugly problem of reality. Historically, the Hebrew Bible emerged out of a real-life environment in which there was no universal legal system for arbitrating disputes and aggression. Violence between peoples was a common and normal fact of life. All the evidence suggests that at least at certain times, the biblical people of Israel had to fight, perhaps even to the death, simply in order to survive as a distinct religious community. Fighting is therefore required at times in the Hebrew Bible because the alternative was perceived as destruction and therefore the inability to carry out the divine will.

But the Hebrew Bible is not Judaism, and Judaism is not the Hebrew Bible. In fact, what we generally call Judaism today is referred to by scholars of religion as *rabbinic* Judaism–the Judaism of the rabbis.

Rabbinic Judaism did not appear until after the period of the Bible. It emerged out of the ashes of the destroyed Jerusalem Temple, the center of biblical Judaism and the symbol of God's power and might. Current scholarship has noted the many parallels between the emergence of rabbinic Judaism and emerging Christianity, both of which grew up in an intellectual and religious environment that combined the great civilizations of the biblical and Greco-Roman worlds.[7]

The great compendium of rabbinic Jewish literature is the Talmud,[8] commonly referred to by rabbinic Jews (that is, virtually the entire Jewish world today) as the "oral Torah." Many outsiders are unaware that for Judaism, the oral Torah parallels in sanctity and importance the written Torah that Jews also call the Hebrew Bible and that Christians know as the Old Testament. Representations of God and the role of humanity found in the Talmud tend to be more consistently quietist, though not pacifist, and exactly as in the case of Christianity, there is a cogent historical reason for this. Both Christianity and rabbinic Judaism emerged after the destruction of the Jerusalem Temple. They materialized as politically and militarily powerless religious/spiritual movements in a world that was under the complete control of the Roman Empire.

While God appears in the Hebrew Bible as a national hero or hero-emperor that saves the nation on the field of battle, rabbinic depictions contrast God with the image of the national hero current at that time.[9]

> The strength of a national hero at the age of 40 is not like what he has at age 50, nor is his strength at 50 like what he has at age 60, nor is it of 60 like 70, for the older he gets the more his strength decreases. But this is not so with the One-Who-Spoke-And-The-World-Came-Into-Being. Rather, "I am the Lord, I do not change" (Malakhi 3:6) . . . When the arrow leaves the hand of a national hero he cannot call it back. Not so the Holy One. Rather, when Israel goes against His will, He issues an edict, as it were, as it is written (Deut. 32:43) "My sword is lightning."[10] When they repent, He immediately withdraws it, as it is written (ibid.), "My hand holds onto judgment." When a human king goes to war and nearby provinces come to him petitioning him for their needs, they are told: "He is troubled; he is going to war. When he is victorious in war and returns, then you can come back and petition your needs from him." But the Holy One is not so. Rather, "YHV is a man of war" when he wars against Egypt, and "YHV is His name" when he hears the cry of all humankind, as it is written (Ps.65:3): "You are the Hearer of prayer whenever anyone comes [and petitions You]."[11]

The greatness of God is contrasted in this text with what only appears as the strength of a human hero. This is exemplified by the old rabbinic legend of the death of the Roman Emperor Titus, the general that destroyed Jerusalem. God appoints the smallest creation, a gnat, to enter through the nose of the great Caesar to imbed itself into his brain and kill him.[12]

It is quite true that in this story of the gnat, vengeance against the destroyer of Jerusalem is at issue. In fact, God is portrayed repeatedly in rabbinic literature as one who would eventually avenge the enemies of Israel, a clear parallel with biblical theologies. But these representations do not occur in "real time." God's vengeance on behalf of Israel is fantasy and occurs in some vague future. The stories are carefully constructed so as not to appear as if Jews themselves can take up arms against their enemies as had the great warrior chiefs known in the Bible as the Judges, or the warrior kings of Israel such as David.

In the Talmud, the countless biblical references to Israel's seemingly ubiquitous sacred wars fought with God, by God, and always for God, are melted down into one paragraph, which, given the Talmudic rhetorical tendency, is an extraordinary feat. Because of the particular nature of the Talmud, there is a visual and chronological break between two parts in the tractate called *Sota,* but they are constructed as one.

In Mishnah *Sota* 8:7, dated to approximately 200 C.E., a long discussion can be found that treats the military deferments listed in the Bible in Deuteronomy 20. The very last paragraph of the discussion ends with: "To what does all the above refer? To discretionary wars, but everyone must go out [to fight] in commanded wars, even a bridegroom from his chamber and a bride from her wedding canopy."

The discussion continues in the second part of the Talmud, called the Gemara and redacted some two or more centuries after the Mishnah. The Gemara continues the discussion as a commentary on the Mishnah sentence "To what does all the above refer?"

> Raba said: The wars of Joshua to conquer [Canaan] were considered required (or commanded) according to everybody. The wars of the House of David for territorial expansion were considered discretionary according to everybody. Where they differ is with regard to [preemptive wars to] reduce the number of idolaters so that they

would not march against them. One calls these commanded, while
the other calls them discretionary. What is the conclusion [from
this difference of opinion]? Whoever is engaged in the performance
of a divine commandment is exempt from the performance of another
divine commandment.[13]

In this remarkable passage, the rabbinic authorities (and it is clear
that this can be safely considered the consensus of the rabbis) cata-
logued the extraordinarily varied and complex biblical expressions
of war into two simple categories. They then put them in the deep
freeze. First, in the Mishnah they applied a simple taxonomy of A/B:
divinely commanded wars (which we would call "holy war" in our
language) and discretionary wars. Only centuries later in the Gemara
did they feel the need to supply an example of each type and a third
category. They could have done much more, and indeed did "complexify" a huge number of other less pronounced biblical institutions.
But war they seem desperately to have wished to leave alone.

Why they did so appears simple enough: too dangerous. It was
too terribly dangerous for a community with no hope of gaining
power over its enemies in "real time" to contemplate actually going
to war. It was too terrifying to contemplate another war after two
famously futile and disastrous attempts to rebel against Rome—
acts that were determined by most of the survivors in retrospect
to have been foolhardy fantasies resulting in death and destruction
that could find precedent only in the prophetic laments over the
bloody massacres perpetrated in the Babylonian destruction of the
first Jerusalem Temple.

As a result of this rabbinic consensus in combination with the
realpolitik of Jewish history, Judaism remained a quietist religious civilization from the end of the second century onward for nearly two
thousand years. Judaism has had quite a consistent record. The rabbis' exegetical management of scripture succeeded in keeping divinely
sanctioned war out of the repertoire of rabbinic Judaism aside from
the realm of fantasy.

There are exceptions to every rule, and some Jewish expressions did indeed include a militaristic-messianic component, but
these were not mainstream, and almost always not rabbinic forms of
Judaism. The military exploits of Abu Isa al-Isfahani and the Isawiyya
movement, for example, were exceptions and quite rare.[14]

Messianism is indeed a central element of rabbinic Judaism, but Jewish messianism tended to be seen as an imminent yet future phenomenon that could not be activated by human volition, and certainly not through militarism. This point is best exemplified by the famous interpretation of the biblical *Song of Songs* found in the Talmudic tractate *Ketubot*. The key phrase is "do not wake or rouse love until it is wished." "Waking or rousing love" is a code for the rabbis of the Talmud to refer to engaging in acts of Jewish political and military self-determination. "Until it is wished" refers to the indecipherable time when God will decide to send the messiah. According to this authoritative rabbinic interpretation, Jews are forbidden to attempt to gain sovereignty through their own actions. God will decide when it is right to send the redemptive messiah, a messiah who will redeem the Jews from the pain and suffering of exile and bring the Jewish people back to their land, the Land of Israel.

To summarize, biblical Judaism appears to have quite a bloody military record. Rabbinic Judaism has virtually none. Simple historical contextualization suggests a simple and logical reason for this great about-face in Judaism. Rabbinic Judaism remained quietist and innocent because it was rendered absolutely incapable of being militant. Today, as a whole, Jews appear to be no less and no more militant religionists than Muslims or Christians. Historically and until only recently, Jews simply could not engage effectively in militant activism.

While today Muslims are perceived and condemned in the West as the most problematic among the three Abrahamic religions on the scale of violence and warring, Professor Fathi Osman has written elsewhere in this volume a persuasive chapter discussing the issues behind this perception. I wish only to add that Islam, like biblical Judaism, emerged out of an environment in which it was required to fight in order to survive.[15] Rabbinic Judaism and Christianity, on the other hand, emerged out of an environment in which they were required to *refrain* from fighting in order to survive.

From the perspective of the academic study of religion and war, one of the most interesting phenomena to observe is the success of certain Christian religious thinkers, after Christianity's spectacular accession to political and military power in the fourth century, in subverting the mostly quietist material of the New Testament in order to justify Christian militarism.[16] My purpose here, however, is to discuss and critique Judaism rather than Islam and Christianity, and I will conclude with an examination of the way in which *Jewish* religious thinkers were able to subvert the largely quietist and antimilitant material of the Talmud in order to justify modern Jewish militarism.

Jews and Judaism lived mostly unempowered and quietist for nearly two thousand years. Without a this-worldly protective power, the deepest piety could not protect the Jews from the will and the willfulness of the powers under which they lived. The one and only time that a community of Jews attained actual self-rule since the Roman destruction of the Jerusalem Temple is the present time in the Jewish state of Israel.

The modern nation-state of Israel is a product of a nexus of forces: historical, political, secular, and religious.[17] Its real founders were secular, not religious, Jews,[18] who did not consider themselves bound by either the Bible or the Talmud. A few Orthodox Jews followed along, but they were not the fathers and mothers of modern Israel. However, once they considered themselves and were considered by the state to be its citizens, they needed to decide whether they could break the 1,900-year ban on the military. There was a great need for their participation in the Israeli army, and there was a great desire among many of them to participate in it.

Even after the establishment of the state, the issue was hardly debated in the small Orthodox Jewish community of Israel. Some Orthodox Jews agreed to join the Israeli forces. Most did not. But something happened after the June 1967 war that signaled a paradigm shift for traditional Jews throughout the world. Whatever the actual intent behind Egyptian president Nasser's very public threats to destroy Israel in May 1967 and massacre its Jewish citizens only two decades after the Holocaust, the Jewish world was terrified that it would actually happen. Communal fasting was called for in the ultra-Orthodox communities. Some wore sackcloth and ashes. The entire Jewish world trembled. And then "redemption" came.

Miraculously, all would say, the Israeli air force destroyed the combined air forces of all five belligerent nations on Israel's borders. And in six days, Israel not only doubled its territory—and this is a key issue—but it captured almost all the villages, cities, and valleys that are mentioned in the Bible. Prior to 1967, Israel was confined largely to the area of ancient Philistia and had little physical connection with the ancient Israelite lands of the Bible. In six days, it regained its biblical patrimony.

All considered it miraculous. But many in the traditional Jewish world believed beyond the idiom. They considered it truly a divine miracle. Was this God rousing the divine love? Was the Holocaust destined to be the last of the great sufferings of the Jewish people? Many considered this to be the case. The 1967 June War became a watershed that, for the first time, enabled the religious Orthodox Jewish world to become outwardly supportive of Zionism–Jewish nationalism. Its impact was immediate, as can be witnessed by the lead article in the main mouthpiece of the community of Orthodox religious nationalists living in Israel.

Everyone who reads the newspapers today, everyone who listens today to the radio . . . is witness to the powerful eruption of faith in the Rock of Israel and its Redeemer. . . . Rabbi Shelomo Goren,[19] the "anointed [priest] of battle"[20] who went before his armies in the conquest of the city of Gaza, who burst into the Ancient City [of Jerusalem] with a Torah scroll in his hand while the bullets were still splitting the air, who announced the good news of the redemption of the Land of Israel with a blast of the shofar. . . . And none of the enemy could stand against them (the Israel Defense Forces). All of their enemies [God] put in their hand. Not one of all the good words that God had spoken to the Children of Israel has failed. Everything is coming to be! And so all the human accounting over the State of Israel according to its 1948 borders has been demolished. Indeed, we have succeeded, but not by our own merit, to witness another stage on the way to Redemption. The way to true Redemption—and not merely the "Beginnings of Redemption." Indeed, every single thing that was written about the words of our prophets is true and enduring, and everything that has not come about by our day will come about before our eyes, before the eyes of all Israel. On the condition: if we are fitting for it "today if you will heed My voice."[21] The Land of Israel is Ours[22] And if we consider all the events [of the past weeks] as revelation of the will of God, then we are not free to return even one handful of land, for we have a legal promissory document regarding it in the Torah and [books of] the Prophets. . . . It was not only

the Israel Defense Forces that established the State and not only
the conquerors of Canaan that prepared the way.... "For You have
given us power to succeed greatly."[23] ...We have merited living in
this epoch in which God has returned to His people and has fulfilled
His word, redeeming His people from the hand of those who are
stronger. And He will redeem us again before the eyes of all the
living, to be our God. And our eyes have seen it! [24]

The writer of these words was neither violent nor militant. Nor
were most of his readers, though over the years many of their children did become increasingly militant over what they considered
the divine promise of the land. Articles and analyses followed in
newspapers, magazines, religious journals, and journals of Jewish religious law. Deeply religious people tried to make sense of the miracle in theological terms and then drew the necessary policy conclusions. There was no single answer, and there continues to be much
discussion and debate even today in the Orthodox world. It is important to understand that militant neomessianism is not the only view
among Israeli Jews. In fact, it is a minority view, but the power of
neomessianism extends far beyond the nationalist Orthodox communities, both within and outside the borders of the State of Israel.
As you can imagine, it resonates deeply, especially among the religious and observant. Although not by any means a universal position, even among the Orthodox, a general consensus has long been
reached by a highly invigorated sector of the Orthodox religious
nationalist establishment.

According to this line of thinking, the 1967 June War (and in retrospect, also the 1948 War of Independence) proves that the gift of
enabling the Israeli army's conquest of Israel's biblical patrimony is
God's one and only offer to the Jewish people to fulfill the divine
promise of Redemption. The result is a new test. The people of Israel
will be redeemed now only if they demonstrate their love of God
by obeying the divine command: the command of reconquest. To
those who believe this, their engagement in violence against Palestinians is not random or cynical acts of human violence. It is part of
milchemet mitzvah–divinely commanded war as learned from the Bible
and Talmud–and it has cosmic significance. Success will bring no less
than divine redemption. But failure will bring on God's anger and
yet another destruction.

What has been narrated here is the story of a religious civilization's transition from a position of relative power to powerlessness, and then a return to relative power. From the standpoint of the student of religion, the story is a fascinating example of how scriptural interpretation responds to the realities of history. Like all scriptures, the Hebrew Bible consists of a wide variety of texts that can be rallied to support a range of positions on many subjects. Interpretive political conclusions can and have ranged from radical militancy to radical quietism.

But from the standpoint of the religious person—not the academic—the story raises very difficult questions about religion. Is everything relative in religion? Even the taking of human life? Does this mean that we must abandon religion altogether in order to be ethical?

Are we as human beings, whether religious or not, destined to abandon nonviolent means of solving pressing political problems the moment we possess power? And are we destined to become a target when we do possess some power?

Despite the range of texts and interpretations on the issue, there is one ultimate message, according to Judaism, that God teaches about war and peace. That message is always "seek peace (or amity) and pursue it." But Judaism recognizes the need to balance between ultimate and competing goods. The need to balance results in a certain relativization of the ultimate requirement of peace. This is both a weakness and a strength in the Jewish way of doing business. It makes arriving at single ultimate and universal conclusions almost impossible. It forces a distinct and individual evaluation of every situation. It tends to "complexify" issues, recognizing that, because life is not simple, our responses to the vicissitudes of life must not be simple either.

There always remains the possibility of error. There is always the option of retreat from responsibility. Judaism recognizes that human error and human nature may render a wrong decision. It nevertheless requires that humans take responsibility to struggle with difficult issues and be accountable for the results of human action.

The story of Jacob struggling with the angel, or according to some, metaphorically, with God herself, reflects this view. Jacob's name, according to the Bible, was changed to Israel as a result of his struggle, and the new name of Israel became the official name for the Jewish people. In the very midst of the struggle, the divine being says to Jacob: "Your name will no longer be Jacob, but rather *Yisra' El* [he struggles with God], because you struggled with God and with humans and you have prevailed."[25]

The greatest struggle for Jews today is reflected in the moral challenge set before us all, Jew and non-Jew alike, in the twenty-first century. It is easy to cry out for peace and justice when excluded from authority. The real challenge is this: when we are in a position of power, can we carry out the vision of peace?

NOTES

1. "Judaism" in this simplistic binary equation usually means the militant expressions of the Hebrew Bible/Old Testament. Marcion seems to be the source of the wrath/love dichotomy (see G. Wilson, *Related Strangers: Jews and Christians 70–170 C.E.* [Minneapolis: Augsburg Fortress, 1995], 207–21). Although Marcion's official stance regarding the total rejection of the Hebrew Bible was not accepted by establishment Christianity, his binary sentiments have remained in various forms and expressions of Christianity to the present. (I am grateful to Professor Mary C. Boys for our e-mail conversation on this topic.)

2. Out of respect and awe associated with the name of God in Jewish tradition, the actual Hebrew four-letter name, sometime referred to as the tetragrammaton and written throughout Jewish Scripture, is neither casually written out nor articulated orally. A number of conventions may be used as a substitute. "YHW" is one of these. Although I take responsibility for all translations here, I am guided by the New Jewish Publication Society translation.

3. And God has his armies (Ex. 12:41, 7:4; 1 Sam. 17:26, etc.). The epithet "Lord of Hosts" is found in the Hebrew Bible 246 times.

4. R. Firestone, "Conceptions of Holy War in Biblical and Qur'anic Tradition," *Journal of Religious Ethics* 24 (1996): 801–24.

5. Jewish Publication Society, 1985.

6. Isaiah 2:4, Micah 4:3.

7. James Parkes, *The Conflict of the Church and the Synagogue* (New York: Atheneum, 1979); John Gager, *The Origins of Anti-Semitism* (New York: Oxford, 1985); Marcel Simon, *Versus Israel* (London: Littman Library, 1996); Daniel Boyarin, *Dying for God* (Stanford, Calif.: Stanford University Press, 1999).

8. The authoritative Rabbinic literature transcends the bounded texts of what is officially named "The Talmud," and includes the genre known as Midrash.

9. E. Urbach, *The Sages,* 89–90.

10. Or, "when my sword is wet. . . ."

11. *Mekhilta of Rabbi Ishmael, Beshalah, Shira.*

12. BR 10:7; ARN (2) 7; Urbach, *The Sages,* 92; and Louis Ginzberg, *Legends of the Jews,* vol. 5, 60 n.191. Similar gnat legends turn up in different guises also in Christian and Muslim literatures.

13. *Sota* 44b.

14. Steven Wasserstrom, *Between Muslim and Jew* (Princeton: Princeton University Press, 1995), 68–82.

15. Reuven Firestone, *Jihad: The Origin of Holy War in Islam* (New York: Oxford, 1999), 9–41.

16. But not entirely quietist. See Stroumsa article.

17. Arthur Hertzberg, *The Zionist Idea* (New York: Atheneum, 1971), 15–100; Israel Bartal, "Responses to Modernity: Haskalah, Orthodoxy, and Nationalism in Eastern Europe," in Shmuel Almog, Jehuda Reinharz, and Anita Shapira, eds., *Zionism and Religion* (Hanover, N.H.: Brandeis University Press, 1998), 13–24; Zalman Abramov, *Perpetual Dilemma* (Jerusalem: World Union for Progressive Judaism, 1976), 55–81.

18. Ehud Luz, *Parallels Meet: Religion and Nationalism in the Early Zionist Movement* (Philadelphia: JPS, 1988).

19. The chief rabbi and chaplain of the Israeli armed forces at the time, and later the Ashkenazic Chief Rabbi of the State of Israel.

20. Mishnah *Sotah* 8:1, Deuteronomy 20:2.

21. Cf. *Shir Rabbah* 5:2, *Pesiqta deRav Kahana* 24:12, *Midrash Tehillim* 95:2, Psalm 95:7, probably with a typo and not intentional.

22. This is a section title in the article.

23. Cf. Deuteronomy 8:18.

24. *Amudim* 256 (June 1967), mouthpiece of the Orthodox Religious Kibbutz Movement, B'nai Akiva, and Torah Ve'avodah, the primary expressions of Zionist Orthodox Jews.

25. Genesis 32:29.

5

Religion as a Force for Reconciliation and Peace: A Jewish Analysis

Irving Greenberg

This chapter was written for presentation at a conference of Christians, Jews, and Muslims. The goal of the colloquy was to help religions become a resource for communities and nations seeking peaceful means of conflict resolution. This objective in itself was a noble response to the widespread recognition that religions around the world are at this very moment, tragically, all too often a source of murderous violence toward people of other religious backgrounds. Religious authority is being used to validate violent ethnic outbursts and to instigate internecine conflicts in many countries. In recent decades, one can point to the religious justifications evoked to pursue genocidal civil war in the Sudan; ethnic cleansing in Serbia and Bosnia; religion-based communal warfare in India, Pakistan, and Northern Ireland; international war between Iraq and Iran; and continuous conflict between Muslims and Jews in Israel and the Middle East. In many other countries, the impact of institutional religion on political and cultural issues has been to escalate them from disagreements subject to negotiation, compromise, and modification to conflicts predicated on nonnegotiable, absolute principles that are resolvable only by the total defeat of the other side (or even by the elimination of the other protagonists). Clearly the organizers of this conference determined to challenge this pattern and to devote their efforts to transform institutional religion from being a source of the problem to being part of the solution.

Religious Violence Desecrates God's Name

One can only honor the motives, the goals, and the efforts of those who organized this conference. Such initiatives are indispensable in our world today not only for the sake of increasing peace and security for all of humanity but also in the hope of reducing what the Jewish tradition calls *chillul hashem*—the desecration of God's name. The truth is that the activity and role of religion in fostering violence bring into disrepute the divine Creator. When the activities of those who preach, teach, and operate in God's name are associated with fanaticism, cruelty, or murder, the divine name is desecrated. Such behaviors reduce the credibility of all religions. Therefore, no religion should be exempt from this effort to stop the violence. Around the world there is a conviction that those who are acting violently are truly driven by religious passion. All religions have become tarnished by the idea that increased devotion to God morphs into claims of absolutism, which easily translate into intolerance and violence.

On the other hand, the implication that all religions are guilty of violence and murder at this moment and that all face equal challenges and obstacles to draw upon their own sources to renounce violence is potentially misleading. Sweeping indictments obscure the complexity of the current reality. All monotheistic religions (one cannot stress this enough, *all*), starting with Judaism (the tradition out of which I speak) as a mother faith, have shown a recurrent capacity to translate the unity and absolute nature of God into a justification of policies that suppress alternative religions and ethical codes, and often do so by violence and war. All the Abrahamic religions have foundational texts that deny the basic validity and even the right to exist of some of the other religions that they encounter. All the Abrahamic religions include texts that justify (or can be used to justify) the expulsion, suppression, or even destruction of those communities that practice other religions. In the past all three have acted out these impulses and drawn upon these texts to justify violence against other faiths or even in some cases against different groups within their own traditions. No Abrahamic religion can afford to be complacent or self-congratulatory. All three religions should avoid the temptation to cite their irenic, constructive, and humane texts as if they constitute the entire tradition.

Nevertheless, one must resist a generalized charge that all faiths aid and abet violence without distinction. All three religions have important elements in their traditions that have been deeply chastened, both by past misbehavior and by current malevolence; therefore, they have begun to question violent behavior or to challenge texts of terror in their own tradition. There are many methods for interpreting classic texts in distinctive ways that neutralize them or limit their ability to justify aggression. New techniques have been actively developed ranging from policies that renounce political power so as to prevent religious groups from exercising force, to active programs of dialogue and peacebuilding, and to reduce hostility and to bring the other into the circle of human dignity that we maintain for our own community. None of the religions is as free as it once was to unself-consciously posit its own self-evident superiority and its right to suppress others without running into opposition, both internal and external.

Having said all this, one must stop and evaluate each Abrahamic faith as to its relationship to others, as to where it is now, as to the indices of violence or power, of suppression or tolerance or pluralism in dialogue. There are significant individual differences among the three. The statement must be made not to offer invidious comparisons but to help diagnose where each faith community needs not only its own efforts but the help of others to shift effectively its behavior from violence toward peace. Each of the major faiths has a serious stake in the others. It is all the more important for all groups to identify accurately what the problems are, what the sources of difficulties are, and how representatives of a particular faith can play a constructive role in strengthening those forces within the other faiths that move it to the side of peace. In the end, no outside religion can correct another. However, the behavior, attitudes, and judgments of outside religions and the extent to which they make themselves more attractive, more loving, and more connected strengthen the internal forces within each faith that are needed to achieve the purification that is our common goal.

A Comparison of the Abrahamic Faiths

Let me then first draw a comparison before I turn to the specifics of my own tradition and where I think the work needs to be done. At the present time, nowhere in the world is Judaism the official religion of a community or of a country where in fact authorities of this faith exercise political and military decision-making power. For the moment, Judaism is not a religion that is the official source of the philosophy of a controlling group or of a leadership cadre that is deciding whether to make political or military attacks upon others. There are within the State of Israel groups such as the followers of Meir Kahane, who have invoked classic religious texts of terror to validate assaults on Arab populations both internal and external to Israel. However, these groups are deeply marginalized. Their own party has been declared racist by law and disqualified by the Israeli Supreme Court from offering candidates in elections. The Kahanists are condemned by the overwhelming majority of the Jewish population of the land of Israel. There is also a political leadership within the National Religious Party (NRP), perhaps the most important mainstream Orthodox religious party in Israel, which is at the present time open to or supporting the concept of transfer, which is nothing less than forced population exchange or ethnic cleansing of Palestinians. Still, they have not been able to establish this concept as party policy. In the elections for NRP leadership in 2002, Effi Eitam, despite being a new figure and a very popular general, had to overcome personal past statements that could be interpreted as supportive of transfer. He had to renounce those statements publicly and pledge not to act on them before he was allowed to complete his candidacy for head of the party and then be able to serve as a member of the government.

For its part, Christianity has been used in part or in whole as a justification for violent policies in the name of religion in smaller, more marginal countries such as Ireland or within Serbia. That having been said, only in these smaller countries has there been anything close to a situation in which Christians with direct ruling authority (in terms of religious or military leaders exercising decision-making power), wrapping themselves in sectarian clothes, have

practiced communal violence and/or ethnic cleansing in the name
of the religion. In major Western countries, where Christianity is
overwhelmingly present and influential, there is no dominant or
leading political group that has used Christianity as its central authority source in pursuing such policies.

Islam is living through a historical crisis now. In a number of major
Islamic countries, governments are practicing or threatening violence, in the name of Islam, against other governments or other communities. (One can argue whether the governments are making a
legitimate use of the religion's name.) The defense of Islam has been
used as the excuse to validate genocidal wars such as Iraq's attacks
on its Kurds and highly destructive wars such as the war between
Iran and Iraq. At the present time there are well-armed and well-
organized terrorists, gaining important support from significant spiritual leaders, practicing violence and terror and justifying it in the
name of the Muslim religion.

This comparative finding is not necessarily a compliment to
Judaism and Christianity as religions vis-à-vis Islam. The dominance
of modernity and modern values, specifically of liberal and secular
values, in the heartland countries of these two religions accounts
more than anything else for the constructive behavior just described.
In all countries where Jews survive as a living community, modernity supplies the dominant set of values. A majority of the Jewish
population of these countries has adopted liberal, humane, and humanitarian values to the point that if they had to choose between any
fundamentalist or religious-text-based call for violence in the name
of the religion and their own modern, liberal values, they would
choose the latter every time. The same holds true in terms of Christianity. By contrast, in Islam's case, in the heartland countries of Islam,
modernity and democracy are both weak. Muslims have been exposed
to democracy and have internalized those values primarily in Muslim minority status countries such as in western Europe, the United
States, and India. As a result, however, the capacity for fundamental
critique of the past and the process of challenging the exclusion-
ary or violence-justifying texts within the tradition by countering
them with universal categories is still weak. The use of classic texts to
unself-consciously validate superiority, suppression, or violence toward
other faiths is still not challenged enough. This needed fundamental

critique (which initially is generated from without as much as from within) has not yet achieved equivalent effectiveness within Islam. One must not make light of the significant renewal and reform movements or the groups offering internal criticism and working for moral purification and for peace within Islam. Still, the relative distribution of power is very different in Islam in no small measure because of the relative weakness of modernity.

This brings us to one of the key methodologies that promises to remove religion as a source of violence. There has been an amazing decline in murder, violence, pogrom, and assault on others in terms of religious behaviors in the twentieth and twenty-first centuries. I want to point to the work of H. J. Rummel on government-sponsored violence and mass murder. Rummel has reviewed the ten largest mass murders of the twentieth century. They involve a wide variety of locations, types, victims, forces, and so on. All ten have one characteristic in common. None of them was carried out by a democracy. This suggests that religious-sanctioned violence may be tamed and murderous group behaviors significantly restricted by democratic process and democratic practices. The division of authority, the creation of checks and balances, the neutralizing effects of countervailing political, economic, and cultural forces unleashed by the democratic process act in concert to stop the practice of organized violence. The key religious question is how to bring democracy into religion, and how to bring religion into democratic process and democratic teaching. This is a methodology that all three Abrahamic religions should be reflecting upon deeply.

IMPROVING ATTITUDES TOWARD THE OTHER AND PREVENTING VIOLENCE: THE CASE OF JUDAISM

Let me turn now to Judaism itself and deal with the central question of preventing violence. What tendencies does one find in the tradition? What methods can one adopt that can be used to teach and model peaceful policies? How can one develop checks on religiously sanctioned violence for which the tradition has been a source in the past? I confess that in trying to present Judaism, one could take almost any position and successfully document it. Jewish tradition

ranges widely. The Bible includes significant, extended passages in
which monotheism's rejection of idolatry is invoked to justify wars
not only of conquest but of annihilation. By contrast, the medieval
rabbinic tradition goes almost to the opposite extreme in suggesting that any use of human force or power is inherently violent and
therefore morally inappropriate. Take the text of Exodus 2:13. At the
opening of Moses' career, Moses sees two Jews fighting. Seeing
one about to strike, Moses says to him, "Wicked one, why will you
hit your neighbor?" The rabbinic interpretation of that text is that
the mere fact of raising a hand turns one into a wicked person, by
definition. Any use of force is inherently evil. On a spectrum ranging from genocidal war to the renunciation of defensive anger, what
position does one choose as the truly representative view of the religion? I offer a somewhat arbitrary selection of three approaches that
exemplify the potential of Judaism to suppress violence; perhaps these
models can be applied by other faiths as well.

UTILIZING CLASSIC TEXTS

Religions can stimulate moral obligation as well as generate and
command love of fellow human beings even as they can be the source
of degradation of the other. The historical problem has been that the
humanistic moral values all too often end up being applied to the
"in" group, to the believers, to those who practice a certain way and
to those who share a certain set of religious assumptions. The excluded,
the others, are not infrequently degraded; their exercise of a different religion or a different religious approach is used as proof that
they are in fact evil. If one goes far enough, the others are deemed
to be less than human in their behavior and therefore open to rejection, exploitation, or even destruction. To move away from violence,
one must expand the context of the universal dignity principle
and thus validate the independent integrity of the lives of others. To
transform values a religion must be persuasive to its own believers;
it can move them best if it can draw upon its own traditions, its own
resources, and its own authority. Therefore, one must seek those core
teachings, those classic foundational texts that if expanded and taught
properly can apply to the broadest framework of humanity. Then

one can actively affirm that the principles of dignity, love, and responsibility apply to those of other faiths as well.

In the words of the great teacher Ben Azzai, as stated in the Jerusalem Talmud (Nedarim ch. 9), the central core teaching of Judaism is that the human being is created in the image of God (Genesis 1:27; 5:1; 9:6). This means that the human being is that form of life that is godlike in its capacities, that is, the human heart, mind, and power are godlike (Psalms 8). In the Babylonian Talmud (Sanhedrin 37A), the Talmud interprets the implications of the creation of the human being in the image of God in another foundational way. As life grows and becomes more and more godlike, life develops dignities. In the end, when human life becomes the image of God, it attains the highest fundamental dignities; these are intrinsic dignities that are neither negotiable nor dependent on the specific physical or spiritual attainments of the individual involved.

There are three fundamental dignities of the image of God. The first is infinite value. Images created by man have finite value. Even the most valuable and precious works of art have finite values. (A Van Gogh painting once sold for $82.5 million.) However, the image that is created by God has infinite value. That is why "to save one life is like saving an entire world." Since the one individual has infinite value, then one has saved an infinity. Saving one infinity is the equivalent of saving six billion times infinity as well.

The second dignity of the image of God is equality. There are preferred human images; a Van Gogh is worth more than an artwork by a Greenberg (and for good reason!). Yet, by definition there is no preferred image of God. In the end all representations of God— whether a young warrior (Exodus 15:3) or a loving mother (Isaiah 66:13; 49:15)—are legitimate representations of God, as long as one does not claim that one is superior to the other. The very claim that there is a preferred image of God is a form of idolatry. God is neither male nor female, neither white nor black, neither Jew nor gentile. It follows that all images of God are equal.

Finally, the image of God is unique. Human images can be replicated and reproduced in identical form. But all images of God are unique. Not even identical twins are identical. It is a defining characteristic of the wondrous handiwork of the Creator that only God can create a creature that is so unique that not a single one is identical to another. If they are properly perceived, all humans are recognized in their uniqueness. This is the test of whether one sees other humans as images of God. Every human being is born with these three fundamental dignities; every human being is entitled to the recognition of his/her dignities, independent of his/her bank account, political status, color, gender, race, or creed.

These three dignities are intrinsic, but also interactive. Properly recognized, they evoke the obligation to protect and to save life. Thus, if one truly, emotionally encounters the infinite value of the other, this stimulates a powerful inner urge to save that life, for that life is infinitely precious. Experiencing others' equality and uniqueness elicits the desire to protect them. If one truly internalizes the value of equality, then one understands that the other has the right to justice and not to be discriminated against even if the other has less money, less access to legal representation, or is somehow outside the official pale. Recognition of equality triggers the sense of the right to a fair share—not to be hungry, not to be poor, not to be oppressed. Similarly, if one recognizes the dimension of uniqueness not as an intellectual construct, but out of emotional response to the uniqueness of the person, then this encounter summons up the sense of obligation to offer what special help this person needs when he or she is sick, or handicapped, or middle class. If the other has a particular yearning for an unmet need, then one wants to help fill the need.

In a like way, the recognition of uniqueness validates the variety of religious or cultural expression, for only such diversity can do justice to the uniqueness of all humans. These dignities, emotionally appropriated, evoke all the obligations and all the protections that move us to a policy of respect and peace for the other. These qualities, once experienced, release the feelings of love in each of us and inhibit the capacity to harm or to kill. Therefore, the key to prevent violence and to encourage good behavior is to give priority weight—indeed exalt—classic texts bearing the message of dignity. These texts must be studied and taught and then turned into policy by invoking the presence behind them, that is, the humanity and the inherent dignities found in the other.

The burning pedagogical problem is: how does one accomplish such a universal application of love? Both the in-group of a religion and religious authorities have the tendency to select out the negative features of the other. They then invoke the bad behavior by some or all members of the other community that "justify" exclusion or denial. The task of today is to prevent religion from being the validator of the process of cultural filtering in which the other is presented as degraded morally or politically or as not a member of the community, as in some way not entitled to these dignities. Such prevention would allow the classic positive texts the power to work their own magic.

Throughout human history, religion and moral systems presented themselves as making absolute demands and as representing divine absolute authority. The desire to ensure the correctness of the authority of this religious system was translated into the creation of an "in" group and of a culture and community whose values were self-evidently superior. The voice of the other and the claims of the alternate value systems were heard faintly or not at all. In the absence of legitimate alternatives, the tradition's values/faith authority was relatively easily passed on within the core community. This process validated the temptation to exercise power and force to the point of the destruction of the other. Today one must be ready to risk the loss of authority and be willing to give up the guarantee of transmission in return for protection against those tendencies to dominance and destructiveness, which are the bane of religion.

THE CONTRIBUTION OF COMMUNICATION

This generation has a tremendous advantage if it takes up the challenge of transformation. We are living in a period marked by the development of a highly porous cultural environment in which every faith and lifestyle are able to present themselves. This environment makes it increasingly possible to encounter the other in his or her full humanity. Through the power of communications, humans everywhere are discovering that the presentation of the other in their own tradition has not done justice to the uniqueness, value, or equality of the other. That recognition evokes the love and the awe that the other is an image of God—a creature of dignity and importance whom one must treat respectfully. The widespread fear of media influence and the frequent opposition to broadcast dissemination of alternative lifestyles do not do justice to the positive effect of the communication of the dazzling variety of human behavior. This communication is not a neutral technical accomplishment. The new cultural situation brings about an enormous expansion of recognition of the image of God.

Rather than focus on media as undermining religious authority because it is taking away the values monopoly once held by religious sources, one should acknowledge that the new representations have given fresh dignity to people who hitherto were seen as inferior. People in conditions such as poverty or illness are presented as fully human, which implicitly invalidates the status quo. With the spread of these images of uniqueness and dignity, the erstwhile victims who had in the past accepted their economically, politically, or culturally second-class status as a given now revolt. Furthermore, the beneficiaries of advantage no longer feel their superiority is as self-evident or valid. In the past, the cultures of the "inferior" were seen as secondary or degraded, which justified the bad treatment by practitioners of the "superior" faith. At best, the excluded values were presented only in a very limited way in the host or central culture. Now these messages, overflowing all barriers, bring the hitherto excluded cultures forward as dignified contexts for distinguished human beings. The main outcome is a worldwide rise in claims of equality, value, and uniqueness by hitherto secondary groups, be they of women, people of color, those who are poor, gay people, or people of minority religions, such as Sikhs or Bahá'í or Sunni in Shiite lands or Shiites in Sunni lands.

The process of moving toward peace rather than violence is greatly stimulated by bringing one's own texts to the table as sources of recognizing universal dignity. The impact of those texts is considerably strengthened by the encounter with the fullness of the humanity of others through the media. This offers religion an opportunity to work with this new cultural tide of communication rather than fighting to suppress the phenomenon or taking it as a threat to individual religions' authority. Religions must give up the past "self-evident" sheltered authority to stop the classic abusive behavior of religion, that is, asserting human value but then revoking it from the particular other by excluding the other from the human category. In the past, exclusion paved the way to legitimate hostility, aggression, and murder. One should note that secular religions of the twentieth and twenty-first centuries have operated in the same fashion.

It is striking that the Nazis, before they carried out their mass killing of the Jews, in order to remove the moral revulsion that individual Nazis would have at the killing of human beings, had to first demonize the Jews. This demonization took many forms. Sometimes the propaganda presented Jews as plotters in a worldwide conspiracy, as underminers of racial purity, or as abusers or sexual predators of children. At other times, demonization took the form of actual behavioral degradation, such as exclusion from citizenship. The Nazis reported Jewish behavior under pressure that was less than ideal as proof that Jews were less than human, when it was the very pressure that the Nazis were exerting that led people to sometimes abandon children or family to save their own lives. In the concentration camps, the system maximized the otherness of the victims by inflicting grotesque uniforms and unsanitary filth on the prisoners. The system operated totalistically, down to the littlest details, including the subtlety of the use of numbers instead of names for inmates, and it continuously used the language of degradation ("shtuck," as in "the Jews are *shtuck,*" or "schiesse," that is, that they are excreta). Nazism illuminates the extent to which degradation of the other can be utilized to justify finally total violence and evil behavior. All religions must learn the lesson and act to prevent even milder forms of abusive violence.

The task of this generation is to ally with the new communication trends to incorporate others in all their status as images of God into the positive central religious categories as creatures worthy of love and help. This is a morally necessary calling, because all cultures are prone to use tactics of denial or degradation of the other. Take the biblical portrait of idolaters: they are inhuman; they practice abominations; they sacrifice children to their idols; they attack and kill weak stragglers; they ask after the dead and practice witchcraft. The total picture is one of a faith that has no validity and of a community that has no dignity; the practitioners are morally unjustified and worthy only of annihilation. Therefore, it is appropriate to uproot and crush every expression of that religion.

The issue is not just biblical. Take the rabbinic variation of *Avodah Zarah*, the portrayal of the idolaters. If one studies the Babylonian Talmud tractate of *Avodah Zarah*, idolaters are presumed in their normal moral behavior to rob and to be capable of killing innocent people for economic advantage or simply for arbitrary reasons. Sexually, they are rapists, homosexuals, and practitioners of bestiality. (This is a composite portrait.) They serve their God Mercules by defecating in front of the idol. Their bizarre behaviors clearly show that their religion has no value. Therefore, one may not enter their holy places; one may not do business with these religions; one may not engage in commerce with idolaters just before their holy days in any way that might advance their religious goals. Their lives are not to be saved on the Shabbat if the effort involves the desecration of Shabbat, although it is the highest commandment in the tradition that one must override Shabbat to save a life. In the classic statement of denigration, the Talmud says that "you are called Adam [human] but the idolaters are not called Adam [human]."[1]

BROADENING THE CONTEXT OF CLASSIC TEXTS

How does one deal with a classic text, which excludes the humanity of the other? Let me offer one example drawn from the very classic source offered as a foundational text for universal human dignity, for example, that the human being is in the image of God and possesses the dignities of infinite value, equality, and uniqueness. There is a conflict between the Jerusalem Talmud, which reports that "he who saves one life, it is equivalent to saving an entire world," and the Babylonian Talmud codified some five hundred years later. After five centuries of exile, pogrom, and exclusion, after Christianity had become the dominant political force persecuting the Jewish people, the text emerges (in the Babylonian Talmud) as: "He who saves one Jewish life, it is the equivalent to saving an entire world."[2] Moral integrity demands that one not make believe there is no problem by always quoting the Jerusalem Talmud. Conversely, one cannot go on giving free rein to those who would quote the Babylonian text to validate indifference to the lives of Arabs in Israel or of other non-Jews.

In the face of such polarity in the foundational text, one can turn to a sympathetic religious authority, such as Rabbi Joseph B. Soloveitchik, perhaps the greatest religious authority of modern orthodoxy in America. Some thirty years ago, Soloveitchik made an unequivocal statement that the image of God status applies to all human beings. After all, in the biblical story of Creation, Adam, the first human, is not a Jew. The story of Adam, which is the source of the image of God dignity, is told in the account of the creation of humanity. It is striking, however, that one of Rabbi Soloveitchik's leading disciples, the teacher who took leadership at Yeshiva University's rabbinical seminary after Soloveitchik, continues to uphold that Babylonian Talmud differentiation and to apply the image of God dignity to Jews, specifically. (Note: Although he has not proclaimed this distinction publicly, he includes it in his teaching.) The lesson is that rarely can a statement by one religious figure, however great, assure the right application of a classic text. Typically, accomplishing a change of categories requires systematic confrontation with the tradition. The process requires the training of new senior scholars; it requires creating a new consensus of authorities that will not tolerate continuing the inherited exclusivity. On this issue, Orthodox Judaism has a way to go. Liberal Judaism has made the unequivocal correction, but it has the advantage of the much more thoroughgoing influence of secular culture on the values of its leaders and followers. There is a separate and distinctive challenge to deal with needed changes within the traditional sector.

Let me cite another example of how to deal with morally problematic texts: how the Talmud comes to grips with the fact that the biblical narrative validates the annihilation of the seven indigenous people of Canaan. This destruction is represented as a positive commandment in the book of Deuteronomy. However, the Talmud stipulates that the seven indigenous nations no longer exist. The Assyrian empire had a systematic policy of mixing populations, deporting locals and bringing in foreigners. Therefore, the Talmud rules that in the aftermath of the Assyrian conquest of Israel, all seven nations became so genetically diluted among other populations that no existent nation can be deemed to fit into the category of being one of the seven.[3] The role of creative interpretation and expansion in dealing with the classic texts is twofold. One may expand the impact and the application of the positive text, or one may narrow, undercut, or make impossible the application of aggressive and destructive texts.

It is particularly valuable to draw on ancient and medieval precedents for the reshaping of tradition, even if these approaches were minority viewpoints in their time. In all candor, *shariah,* canon law, and the internal norms of *halacha* are the areas that are still the least reshaped by modern values, yet there is where the problems often lie. Contemporary decisors in the Abrahamic traditions are more comfortable in following older sources. In this spirit, I offer another helpful precedent for revision of past hostile attitudes toward other religions. Menachem ben Shlomo Meiri (1249–1316), a major medieval Jewish decisor and teacher, rules that all statements about idolatry and idolaters no longer are operative because they applied only to pagans, that is, to members of religions that no longer exist. Says Meiri: Christianity and Islam are deemed to be practiced by people whose ethics and inner morality have been shaped by the process of becoming civilized by religion; that is, their religions have turned them into morally, ethically responsible humans. Therefore, Christians and Muslims are categorized as monotheists, not idolaters. In setting ethical policy vis-à-vis monotheists, one must stipulate that they practice a higher morality. They cannot be treated as idolaters and shown disrespect or mistreated. Meiri's key recognition is that the Christian and Muslim traditions, as independent religions (not just because Christianity is the daughter of Judaism or that Islam has been shaped by Jewish values), have successfully raised generations of people who live by the moral standards of monotheism. Therefore, none of the inherited pejorative terminology and categories can be legitimately applied to members of such faiths.

COVENANTAL METHOD AS A PROCESS OF MOVING BEYOND VIOLENCE

There is a second major model that Judaism can contribute toward ending violence and murder in the name of religion. Judaism's central process, covenant, seeks to unite ideal vision and concrete pragmatic method together to perfect the world. The central ideal of

Judaism, *tikkun olam* (perfecting the world), teaches that God the Creator wants and seeks a perfect redeemed world. God promises that this stage of redemption will be reached eventually. The definition of that perfect world is a world full of life, especially life in the image of God, in which life is accorded all its dignities, including the dignities of infinite value, equality, and uniqueness intrinsic to an image of God. In the Messianic Age, we are promised that the plenitude of dignity will be achieved. Then poverty, hunger, discrimination, war, and indeed sickness and death itself will be overcome. In such a world, violence and all forms of institutional wrongdoing will not exist.

Judaism as a religion teaches that God has promised that this state of the world will be brought into being. This state of perfection will be accomplished for all humans, not just Jews, but it will take a partnership of God and humanity to achieve this goal. However, in the interim, the world is not perfect. Therefore, one must create an ethical code that can deal with the reality of the world as it is while enabling us to work toward upgrading the world and bringing it to that final perfection. The guiding principle of this covenantal process is to choose life as against death. Since the ideal in its purest form— pure life, pure peace—is not available currently, to choose life means to choose those tactics that maximize life, under the circumstances.

In an ideal world, no war would ever be waged. There would be no violence. "They will beat their swords into ploughshares and spears into pruning hooks and learn war no more" (Isaiah 2:4). However, in the present, people are living in an unredeemed world. There are evil people present. There are powerful forces that will use any mechanism (including religion) to advance their evil agenda, up to and including war. Under such circumstances, a war of self-defense can be a moral response and a legitimate tactic. The *halacha* ultimately defines three kinds of war. One is a war of self-defense (over the basic right to exist, basic security), which is categorized as a *milchemet mitzvah* (a "commanded" or a "good deed" war). When war is action in self-defense against a foe who seeks to destroy me, then going to war constitutes a "good deed," not an exercise of violence. There is a second possible case, however, when the war cannot be shown to involve immediate self-defense. There is a threatening enemy; the enemy may attack if one does not preempt. On the other hand, maybe not. There may be other ways to preserve the peace. Maybe in the future the wicked will become strong enough to attack, but maybe other factors will prevent this. Such a situation demands a judgment call. Under these circumstances, the *halacha* ruled that the most one can conclude is that such a war would be categorized as a *milchemet reshut*—a permitted war.

What does it mean to wage a permitted war? There are special restrictions placed on tactics in pursuit of the goal. Restrictions start with requiring that the decision to fight must be approved not only by the executive branch, but by the Sanhedrin, which then constituted both the legislative and the judicial branches as well. Wide-ranging exemptions from army service are permitted to those who do not want to serve in such a war, including those who morally oppose this war. Finally, the military tactics must be even more restrained and restricted, because this war is based on a judgment call. The waging of such a war is inherently more problematic morally, because the campaign is not unequivocally of a defensive character.

There is a third form of war also—an aggressive, unjustified war, which in fact is nothing less than pursuing evil. Waging such a war is sinful and forbidden, for war spills blood. Note that even in defensive war, if one could turn tactically from war to diplomacy, then pursuing the military option no longer constitutes *milchemet mitzvah*. One should also note that even in a commanded war, the returning soldiers who have killed in the course of that war are judged to be ritually impure. They have shed blood even though fighting the war was a mitzvah. The soldiers must undergo ritual purification before they can reenter the sanctuary and rejoin the community. This combination of ideal utopian vision and compromising partial methods of realization is a central approach to restricting excesses in the name of good causes (such as religion).

This analytic method leads us to a crucial distinction. Exercising power and force is not the same as practicing violence. Violence must be defined as an unjustified use of power and force. Not all use of force is violent or wrong. Measured force in defense of life is legitimate. Otherwise, evil that, in our time, has access to unlimited aggressive force and power would triumph unopposed. Death wins out if good people are unable or unwilling to take up arms in defense of life.

To maintain morality and peace, one must continuously make needed distinctions. What is violent, unjustified, or aggressive behavior? What is power that is properly used in limited defense of life? How can one ensure that killing does not become an end in its own sake or unlimited or primarily focused on civilians in a war? A good deed war in which the military would attack civilians primarily would become morally improper. Such a campaign would be even more morally problematic because it harnessed good values such as religion, self-sacrifice, and martyrdom and turned them into a source of justification for cruelty and unjustified violence against the innocent. In the end, religions must observe core distinctions between violence and power—violence is illegitimate and power legitimate—or religions hand over the world to terrorists or even would-be practicers of genocide.

Peace will not be possible until terrorists understand that terrorism will not succeed and give it up as a technique. If one yields to the temptation to abstract principle from tactics, or to weaken resistance to violence on the grounds that it is intrinsic to human nature and inescapable, if one then suggests that the only way to go beyond violence is to offer a pure pacifist response as a moral counterforce to war by asserting a kindness that refuses to fight, then one is guilty of collaboration by handing over the world to evil. As George Orwell pointed out, the tactic of opposing violence with love and civil disobedience carried out in India by Mahatma Gandhi worked because the British occupiers were relatively benign. The English government yielded to civil disobedience. The British revised their policies and eventually withdrew altogether—unlike the rulers under Nazism, Stalinism, and Maoism (and the practitioners of terror in the name of Islam) who used unlimited force to crush the opposition.

PLURALISM AS A MECHANISM FOR PEACE

There is a third approach for which Judaism has resources to strengthen the forces for peace within religion. This would be to build on its traditions of pluralism of power, of influence, and of textual sources. Biblical Judaism divided power between tribes and central government, between monarch and priesthood, and between government officials (including priests) and prophets. Rabbinic Judaism canonized multiple, even contradictory, voices and texts on covenant, on divine justice, on the nature of divine intervention, and so on.

To reduce their violent tendencies, all religions must now take upon themselves the commitment to a thoroughgoing radical pluralism. Religions should insist on pluralism in religious life, and in economic, political, and social life, as well as in culture, to protect against their own totalizing tendencies. Religions can lead the way in taking up the risks involved in sustaining an atmosphere in which every faith and all kinds of lifestyles are available. The risk is that the unrestrained marketplace of ideas and values can lead to a condition of cultural relativism in which no values stand up. The potential gain is that faiths learn to witness effectively in the presence of the full dignity of the other. This would pave the way for a plurality of positive, credible models of faith enriching and correcting each other—and preventing abuse and violence on the part of any one privileged faith.

Pluralism is the only surefire way to achieve a balance of power in which all religions are encouraged to act ethically. The ability to abuse is inherent in lopsided concentration of power—in any form. Ultimately, power is not just political or even military. Power also grows out of cultural force and economic capability. Therefore, all forms of power, including religious, must be balanced. No tradition is free of the potential corruptions of power. Without an equilibrium of power, the potential for evil eventually will be acted out in all traditions. Therefore, it is necessary to affirm the centrality of pluralism and seek a balance of power to bring out and strengthen the forces of peace in each tradition.

There are various ways this prophylactic action has been taken already. The separation of political power and religion, one of the major contributions of modern culture, has helped both Judaism and Christianity in the Western countries to avoid much of the cruelty, violence, and genocide that they inflicted or participated in in the past. Islam and traditional Judaism have many more problems with separating religion and state, particularly because of their conception that all of life should be lived in the religious spirit. Even so, they may nevertheless affirm the separation of religion and state on the grounds that whatever the risk/cost in separating religion from life, it is outweighed by the gain in prevention of inflicting evil in the name of religion. In the words of the psalmist, "depart [remove yourself] from evil, and [then] do good" (Psalms 34:15).

Judaism and Islam may prefer the Israeli, that is, the European, version of separation, which involves not a decisive separation of church and state as in the United States, but rather a kind of multiple establishment. In many European countries, there is an official state religion but this status is extended to all religions in the country. This reduces the exclusion or abuse of minority religions. This approach has not worked perfectly by any means. Once there is a strongly entrenched political authority connected to religion, the religious authorities—especially of the majority religion—try to gain special advantages, frequently at the expense of other faiths. In Israel, the Supreme Court (the so-called secular Supreme Court) has repeatedly intervened to check such excesses or one-sided favoritism. This separation approach remains a particular challenge for Islam because in most of the countries where its adherents are the majority, the Muslim faith is established exclusively. How to separate off or to limit that connection without turning the polity into a pure secularist system is no easy challenge to meet. Still, it will need a special effort to stop the kind of persecution or discrimination in Islamic countries against those who differ within the tradition (as the treatment of Shiites in Saudi Arabia or of Sunnis in Iran), as well as to end the policies of making those who belong to a different faith into second-class citizens (Jews and Christians as *Dhimmis*). Implicit in this approach is a turn of religions toward support for democracy and pluralism in law and in politics even if this reduces religious influence on the society (at least in the short run), and even at the risk of religion becoming privatized. There is a word of consolation one can offer at this prospect. The fact is that in America, religion in a voluntary way has achieved major influence on societal and governmental policies, propagating the very values for which religions try to establish themselves in the government. It may be that the high degree of religiosity in America (much higher than in Europe where religion is established) proves that less is more. At the least, separation and equalization have brought out the best tendencies to peaceful coexistence in the various religions favored in the United States.

In the final analysis, pluralism is not only a good tactic. It is the outgrowth of the recognition that the human being as an image of God is of infinite value and equal. If I am infinitely valuable and equal, do I not have a right to speak? No matter what my view is? Even if in the judgment of others my view is mistaken or wrong? If I am unique, do I not have the right to my own religious context in which I grow? Is this not true no matter how valid the other religion may feel it is, compared to my faith? Therefore, I would offer as a religious criterion that all faiths that show the ability to instill these values (of viewing the human as infinitely valuable, equal, and unique) in their adherents, all faiths that teach believers to honor these dignities—and therefore show their creeds' capacity to raise humans in the image of God—should be judged as valid. All of a religion's additional teachings or specific truths about divine and human should be treated as strengths or weaknesses; however, the need to correct weaknesses cannot invalidate a religion's right to exist. This is the commitment that the Abrahamic faiths should make—not only to each other, but also to other major religions that do not fit the covenantal model.

This pluralist model should be applied to religion, but also to political, cultural, and economic power. The issue, and the policy, transcends the nature of the ruling framework. Note that Jews classically felt that where Christianity and/or Islam was dominant, they would be treated as second-class citizens. Therefore, many Jews (particularly in eastern Europe) joined socialist or communist movements in the belief that only secular, universal equality would finally remove the discrimination factor that led nations to treat Jews as inferior. Yet once communist secularism took full power in the U.S.S.R. and achieved universal control of political and socioeconomic levers, the ruling group turned to persecuting Jews and turned other religious groups into second-class citizens as well. The lesson is obvious: economic or political power, monopolistically held, is no less a source of discrimination and abuse of power. Therefore, one has to support pluralism in economic sources as much as in political or religious institutions. By the same token, there must be pluralism in value systems, in school systems, and in the sources of religious values and authority that characterize each religion. Pluralism is a fundamental prophylactic against violence and abuse.

SELF-CRITICISM AS A FOUNDATION FOR PLURALISM

To achieve successful living together in pluralism will require a commitment on the part of each of the Abrahamic religions to self-criticism and to finding its own limits.[4] In working for pluralism, one must resist falling into the temptation of articulating a relativism in which all values are equally good or equally invalid or equally irrelevant. A true pluralist affirms the absolute commitments within his/her tradition and, at the same time, discerns the faith's limitations. A true pluralist system is simply an absolute system that has come to understand its own limitations. Personally, I believe absolutely that Judaism is the word of God. I believe absolutely that Judaism is an ultimate calling of humans to the service of God. At the same time, I have come to see that my religion has not exhausted God's wisdom. This leaves room for other religions and other cultural behaviors. I believe that my calling was not intended to be the religion of all human beings. How could it be when humans have such uniqueness and variety in their own life backgrounds? This needed sense of limitation is most powerfully expressed in a willingness to self-critique. It also often takes the form of repentance.

Ever since I became deeply involved in the Jewish-Christian dialogue after the Holocaust, I have been struck by the extent to which Christians—influenced by modernity and its critique, but also by guilt over the Holocaust—were motivated to self-critique. My dialogue partners were often driven by the desire to overcome the evil inflicted by Christians upon the Jews in the past. They recognized that that evil climaxed in a grotesque and vile genocide in which the Nazis acted far beyond what Christians ever thought would be done in the name of their traditional teaching of contempt about Judaism. Nevertheless, these good Christians did not seek to evade guilt by pointing out that the Nazis went much further than Christians intended. Out of repentance, Christians have self-critiqued, repudiated supercessionism, and fought to clarify or eliminate anti-Jewish stereotypes. They have labored to reduce or neutralize texts of terror and exclusion. In the process, they have made Christianity into a far more morally effective faith. They have moved it from being a privileged sanctuary of hatred to being a true gospel of love—even to Jews. Christianity's turn shows that repentance and guilt are major sources of the sense of limitation that paves the way to support religious pluralism and internal correction. These feelings make faith more just, more competent morally, more modest in its relation to God, and more humane and peaceful. Paradoxically, Islam's current problem may be intensified in that it does not feel guilty enough. For the moment, the needed critique cannot be supplied from outside. Therefore, it is sad that Muslims have responded to the Holocaust as if it is a Zionist ideological bogey. Because Shoah consciousness strengthens Israel's right to existence, Arab nations and Islamic preachers have become a major source of Holocaust denial. Many other Islamists argue that the Shoah has nothing to do with Arabs. They insist that this genocide is a western European phenomenon whose aftereffects are being inflicted upon the Middle East. One could argue that in fact there is a direct Shoah responsibility on Muslim heads. For example, Arab pressures led to the closing of (then) Palestine; this prevented hundreds of thousands, if not millions, of Jewish lives from being saved. One could even cite the collaboration of the Muslim Mufti of Jerusalem with Hitler. However, that is not the argument on which I would wish to focus. If Shoah is not the source of the appropriate guilt, then Muslims have to find the need for repentance in other sources and Islam's other history. God help us, there is enough evil inflicted in the name of the faith to generate the moral challenge of self-correction.

In the end, repentance is one of the most powerful forces that drives faith not only to correct its own errors but to reconcile one religion with another. A personal witness: Some twenty years ago while wrestling with the implication of the Holocaust, I spoke to my own Orthodox rabbinic colleagues. I had to confess that, in my journey, I had started by criticizing Christianity. Then, in the course of my encounter with Christian self-purification, I came to feel less and less impressed with the Orthodox response to the Shoah. I came to see my own failure to discern my guilt. I had not applied the Holocaust test (never again stereotyping, moral apathy, self-seeking, playing it safe) to my own religious life. I explained to my colleagues that I had come to a stage of repentance in which I felt that it was our responsibility as Orthodox Jews to affirm the dignity and the validity of Christianity and of Islam as well as of the non-Orthodox Jewish denominations (lest we be tempted by our pejorative attitudes to repeat the sin of bystanding in some future crisis). I also made the point that Reform, Conservative, and Reconstructionist Jews had shown no less and no more recognition that the Holocaust was coming than the Orthodox had. During the war, no matter what faith or what version of Judaism one practiced, the view did not change in a consistent way how one dealt with the moral crisis; nor after the war had any of the groups been particularly good at self-criticism.

The presentation was not well received. At the end there was a question-and-answer session. A colleague in the back stood up and said that he was truly offended by my presentation and surprised that an Orthodox rabbi would say these things. After all, the implication of my words was that if we take the Holocaust seriously, in the end there is no difference. Well then, he asked, in light of what I had said: "What should you be after the Holocaust? Orthodox, Conservative, or Reform?" My response was: "After the Holocaust it is not so important whether you are Orthodox, Conservative, or Reform, as long as you are ashamed of it." I thought the response was humorous, but the audience was not amused. In a rage, the man yelled back at me: "So why are you Orthodox?!" I replied: "Because Orthodoxy is the group I am most ashamed of." That was the last time I was invited to speak at my rabbinical colleagues' convention.

I have reflected on this quip many times since. I believe that it contains a profoundly true moral statement. Understand please that I am not ashamed of my faith; I am proud of it. To speak of being ashamed is to say that one has become aware of the limitations of one's religious positions. Because I love it and stake my life on this faith, I have become aware of its flaws and failures. My task is not to validate and justify the errors. My task—the task of all true believers—is to actively search out the faith's flaws in order to stop it from possibly mistreating or degrading the other. Why do I critique Judaism? Because I love it. "The group I am most ashamed of" is another way of saying that I love all human beings; I love all religions; I understand that I have a responsibility to them. I do. However, I have a special responsibility for my own religion. Therefore, I have a special sense of embarrassment when my own tradition lends itself to abuse or if it actively harms others.

If all of us can apply this self-critique to our own traditions, all believers can meet on that field of purification and repentance and become truly reconciled with one another. In the end, religion is simultaneously a source of evil and of violence but also the source of love—the universal infinite love of God. Religion, purified, is the validation of the premise that God and humans together in all our combinations and relationships can make this world a world of peace, love, and mutual responsibility.

NOTES

1. BT Keritot 6B; cp. Soferim ch.15, pa. 10; but also cp. Avodah Zarah 3A and Tosafot bdh Kohanim, loc. cit. One must confront these texts, recognizing that their authority is powerful. One could go through the Christian tradition or the Islamic tradition and find texts equally degrading and equally destructive of the existence of the other. The task is for each practitioner to specialize in his/her own faith, which he/she knows better and has the right to improve. If I were to read counterpart texts in the other traditions, it would sound like an outsider's attack. I leave that effort to the conscience and responsibility of those who practice within each faith.

2. There are earlier texts of the Babylonian Talmud that read "one life" not "one Jewish life."

3. It follows that the application of the policy of annihilation would be immoral and improper.

4. But note that these found limits are parameters of competence and power.

6

Disciples of the Prince of Peace? Christian Resources for Nonviolent Peacebuilding

R. Scott Appleby

Since the end of World War II, I shall argue in this essay, momentum has been developing, within both Christian theology and praxis, toward nonviolent peacebuilding as the heart of the Christian ethic. Today nonviolence is seen by significant numbers of Roman Catholics and mainline Protestants—as well, of course, as by members of the historic peace churches—not merely as an option, but as the nonnegotiable dimension of Christian discipleship. Peacebuilding, as we shall see, is the constructive agenda of the nonviolent agents of social change. First, however, it is necessary to trace the emergence of nonviolence itself as a priority within mainstream Christian communities.

THEOLOGICAL RESOURCES

Among the fundamental theological resources for this development within Western Christianity is the body of work produced by a generation of authors who portray Jesus, the "founder" of Christianity, as the model of nonviolent resistance to the forces of oppression and injustice in the world. In this view the Christian presumption against violence is rooted in the example of Jesus of Nazareth, whom the Church proclaims to be the Word of God made human, "God of

God, Light of Light, true God of true God, begotten not made, one in Being with the Father, through whom all things were made," as the Nicene creed has it—and who was, in his earthly existence, one who rejected violence and refused to resist his executioners. The defining mark of the lived tradition of Jesus, these authors insist, is the fact that he forgave his tormentors at the hour of his death and prayed for their redemption. If God does not retaliate, they ask, how are we justified in doing so?

How, in short, could Christians, so consistently throughout history, reject nonviolence and embrace—even sanctify—war? In rejecting nonviolence, forgiveness, and peacebuilding as a way of life, have they not also rejected *imitatio Christi*—the imitation of Christ—an otherwise hallowed path to holiness and a model of Christian soteriology?

Such questions stand at the center of what we might call an ecumenical theological "school" of nonviolence that has been gaining ascendancy within Christianity, as I mentioned, since the world wars of the twentieth century. In the early years of the twenty-first century, even in the aftermath of the terrorist attacks of September 11, 2001, this theological and ethical trajectory is gaining strength within Christian faith traditions. Historical theologians studying this evolution toward nonviolence include in its trajectory, among others, the Roman Catholics Dorothy Day, Thomas Merton, and Daniel Berrigan; the Mennonite John Howard Yoder; the Methodist Stanley Hauerwas, and the Lutherans Jürgen Moltmann and the Croation-American scholar Miroslav Volf. Volf summarizes the trajectory by quoting Yoder and Moltmann. Yoder: "Only at one point, only on one subject, but then consistently, universally—is Jesus our example: in his cross."[1] Moltmann: "The sufferings of Christ on the cross are not just his sufferings; they are the sufferings of the poor and weak, which Jesus shares in his own body and in his own soul, in solidarity with them."[2]

Tracing the tradition of nonviolence and pacifism, these theologians and ethicists point to the apostolic and subapostolic Christians who, during the first three centuries after Christ's death, refused to serve in the Roman army and adopted nonviolence as a way of life; to the Anabaptists of the Radical Reformation—including the Society of Friends—who embraced pacifism as essential to the *imitatio Christi;* to modern Christian pacifists such as Dorothy Day and

Thomas Merton; to disciples of nonviolent resistance such as Martin Luther King Jr. or the Monks of Tibhirine, martyred for their faith in Algeria, or the Filipino Christian women of Silsilah, who practice nonviolence and dialogue with their Muslim neighbors (and opponents).

The theologians of nonviolence have also devoted considerable energies to refuting their own intellectual and pastoral opponents within the Christian household, including advocates of just war and less critical supporters of the militarist state. The rejectionists (of nonviolence and pacifism) have offered several arguments:

1. Jesus was exceptional, indeed unique—not a model of emulation. He redeemed humankind by his sacrificial death on the cross, not by pursuing a social agenda. The meaning of Christ's death is theological, not ethical—it was a one-and-for-all atonement, not a path to be followed or a model to be imitated by his disciples. Christ's death, that is, was a forensic act, a deed that served to justify others. We experience it today through sacrament and Word, not through ethics.

2. Jesus offered his disciples peace only in the upper room, after his resurrection; it is unrealizable in historical time and space.

3. Jesus mistakenly believed that the Apocalypse was nigh, and so did not worry himself or his disciples about the complexities of ethical decision making in a world where the evil threaten the innocent, for such a world was about to vanish.

4. Jews were a minority unable to take up arms to throw off the oppressor, so Jesus' refusal to fight was pragmatic. Christians living in later, changed circumstances were obligated to answer questions which Jesus did not face. In short, the individual Christian, or Christians together, must accept responsibilities that were inconceivable in Jesus' situation.

5. Jesus' message was ahistorical by definition: he dealt with spiritual, not social, matters, with the inwardness of faith. But we must uphold his truth and values in a fallen world, where might rules and Christendom is not an option but an imperative. (Through this version of will-to-power, the theologians of nonviolence insist, "just war" theory has been applied to serve unjust ends.)[3]

In developing their responses to these objections, the theologians of nonviolence have developed a consensus around the following points:

1. What becomes of the meaning of incarnation if Jesus is not normatively human? If Jesus is human but not normative, Yoder argues, this is the ancient ebionite heresy. If he is authortiative but not in his humanity, this is gnosticism or docetism.[4]

2. According to the biblical witness, Jesus is a model of radical political action. As a result of consensus in scholarship of the Christian scriptures, it is no longer possible to maintain, as mainstream Christianity has for centuries, that the ethic of Jesus was an ethic for an "interim" that Jesus thought would be very brief. It is no longer possible, that is, to hold that Jesus' rejection of violence, of self-defense, and of accumulating wealth for the sake of security are not permanent and generalizable attitudes toward social values.[5]

3. Moltmann, Volf, and others add the trinitarian and cosmological theme of divine self-donation for the sake of the other, characterizing this divine act as central to Christian ethics under the inspiration of the Holy Spirit. Indeed, the reception of enemies into the eternal communion of God is a mark of the kingdom. "Like solidarity with the victims, the atonement for the perpetrators issues from the heart of the triune God, whose very being is Love," Volf writes.[6] "On the cross of Christ, this love [that is, the love of God] is there for the others, for sinners—the recalcitrant—enemies," Moltmann concurs. "The reciprocal self-surrender to one another within the Trinity is manifested in Christ's self-surrender in a world which is in contradiction to God; and this self-giving draws all those who believe in him into the eternal life of the divine love."[7] Christians, by definition, are caught up in this trinitarian relationship of self-donation and receptivity; the ethical expression of this ontological reality is forgiveness of enemies and rejection of revenge.[8]

In response to those who would dismiss the trinitarian metaphysic and the "ethics for enemies" as hopelessly idealistic and utopian, the theologians of nonviolence emphasize the price to be paid, in blood and spiritual suffering, for the praxis of nonviolence and embrace of

the other. Hauerwas has written frequently and without restraint of
the cost of discipleship. Volf, likewise, acknowledges that

> the ultimate scandal of the cross is the all too frequent failure of self-
> donation to bear positive fruit: you give yourself for the other—and
> the violence does not stop but destroys you; you sacrifice your life—
> and stabilize the power of the perpetrator. Though self-donation often
> issues in the joy of reciprocity, it must reckon with the pain of fail-
> ure and violence. When violence strikes, the very act of self-dona-
> tion becomes a cry before the dark face of God. This dark face con-
> fronting the act of self-donation IS a scandal.[9]

This acceptance of the scandal, in my view, marks a maturity in
the Christian theology of peace and nonviolence, and offers an important corrective or balance to the somewhat and sometimes facile cel-
ebrations of "the victory of nonviolent revolutions" in the twentieth century. That is, peace activists and scholars point almost
triumphally to Gandhi's campaign of nonviolence, which drove the
British out of India, and to the nonviolent revolutions in eastern
Europe (Poland and the Czech Republic, in particular) and in the
Philippines, as indicators that nonviolence is now clearly the wave
of the future, that war is obsolete.[10]

Hardly. The disaster in Iraq and the continuing violence in
Afghanistan, Pakistan, Indonesia, the Congo, and Israel/Palestine
make this claim contestable even from within the peace camp. More
insidiously, nonviolence, like other historically contingent human
acts, may have unintended consequences. The historian Judith Brown
titled her critically acclaimed biography of the Mahatma, *Gandhi,
Prisoner of Hope,* in order to reflect her thesis that Gandhi's religious
worldview and ardent commitment to nonviolence ultimately undermined progress toward concrete political goals that might have led
India closer to an actual experience of communal nonviolence.
Brown also argues that the British would have withdrawn from India
in any case, as they realized after the wars that they were hopeless
overextended; Gandhi's nonviolent campaign was less a trigger than
the lore has it.[11] Similarly the *New York Times* journalist Chris Hedges,
among others, has argued that the Christian advocates of nonviolent revolution in eastern Europe—the so-called peacemakers in

East Germany and the Czech Republic were irrelevant at best, and often feckless.[12]

My point here is not to dismiss the political effectiveness of non-violence, merely to note that it can be of limited efficacy and that the Christian commitment to it does not promise empirically specifiable results or an absence of sacrifice and often brutal suffering on the part of the practitioners. Hence Volf and company add an important element of realism to the emerging theology of nonviolent peacemaking.

ECCLESIAL AND INSTITUTIONAL RESOURCES: ROMAN CATHOLICISM AS A CASE STUDY

Does the movement toward Christian nonviolence extend beyond the small group of theologians and ethicists sampled above? Evaluating institutional responses requires a different calculus. Major religious traditions are internally plural and therefore not given to the kind of monolithic presence that is often ascribed to them. Yet trends develop within the theological schools and praxis heads in discernible directions. Moreover, the idea that religions evolve and reinterpret their mission takes on special significance in an era of globalization. The extension and improvement of cross-cultural communications and transportation, the continual migration of peoples that is no longer impeded by vast spaces to traverse across regions and continents, and the resulting acceleration of the process by which religious actors absorb and integrate exogenous cultural and ideological elements—all this has led to a religious polycentrism unmatched in previous eras. Particularly within the great traditions unregulated by a centralized government or lacking a hierarchy with comprehensive executive, juridical, or legislative powers—but not only in these religions—one sees a proliferation of para-ecclesial movements, groups, and spokespersons claiming the authority of the great tradition for their special form of advocacy and activism.

To some observers the intensity of this disengaging and reengaging process means that religions are fragmenting and squandering the power that comes with purity and uniformity. To others, however, the proliferation of subtraditions, intentional religious communities, and religious NGOs represents an enormous opportunity to mobilize the resources of the religious traditions for peacebuilding.

These contradictory attitudes are found, for example, within most modern religious communities, not least in Roman Catholicism, whose 1.2 billion members make it Christianity's largest church body. By the end of the twentieth century, the Catholic Church had repositioned itself vis-à-vis the state and civil society, retreating from entangling alliances with the former to assume a constructive and sometimes prophetic role within the latter. At the same time and as a result, the church has produced significant lay and clerical religious movements and NGOs that display great promise as religious peacebuilders. The vibrant internal pluralism of the Christian tradition made possible the Catholic transformation from proponent of theocracy to major player in pluralist civil society and champion of democracy.

In a striking twentieth-century reversal, Roman Catholicism abandoned its previous claims to political privilege, renounced the theocratic model of political order, and became a powerful proponent of religious liberty and universal human rights. This "development of doctrine," ratified in 1965 during the final session of the Second Vatican Council (1962–65), was a dramatic example of internal religious pluralism turned to the advantage of ecumenism, tolerance, human rights, and peace. The retrieval and official endorsement of a liberal doctrine of religious freedom was a decisive moment in the evolution of modern Roman Catholic social doctrine, a body of teachings on the social order inaugurated by Pope Leo XIII's 1891 encyclical, *Rerum Novarum* (The Condition of Labor), the first in a long line of papal, episcopal, and conciliar documents that established and refined the basic tenets of the Catholic social tradition.[13]

Catholic social teaching, in turn, forms the foundation of contemporary Roman Catholic political philosophy; it constitutes the official frame of reference for Catholics exercising their rights and responsibilities in the public order. Moreover, Catholic social teaching articulates a *religious* duty of Catholics: the documents of the Second Vatican Council—especially *Gaudium et Spes,* the *Pastoral Constitution on the Church in the Modern World*—and the social encyclicals of Pope John XXIII (1958–63 as pope), Pope Paul VI (1963–78) and Pope John Paul II (1978–), place social teaching at the center of Roman Catholic self-understanding, ecclesiology, and pastoral practice.

It is difficult to overstate the depth and scope of the ecclesial transformation that occurred over the course of the twentieth century. Until 1965 Roman Catholicism had legitimated the denial of civil and other human rights to non-Catholics by teaching, in effect, that "theological error has no rights" in a properly governed (that is, Roman Catholic) state. The second quarter of the nineteenth century was a defining moment in the initial phase of Catholicism's "internal argument" over the proper role of religion in the modern state. Faced with a popular uprising in Rome and the papal states, the newly elected Pope Gregory XVI (1831–46 as pope) stood firmly against calls for elected assemblies and lay-dominated councils of state. In the encyclical *Mirari vos* (1832), he denounced the concepts of freedom of conscience, freedom of the press, and separation of church and state, the liberal ideas associated with the French priest Félicité de Lamennais and his newspaper *L'Avenir*. Lamennais also held that the common consent of all humanity was a norm of truth. Gregory XVI, by contrast, accepted the basic assumptions of neoscholastic ecclesiology that the clericalized, monarchical structures of the church were divinely mandated, and he believed that they were to be duplicated in the temporal order. Accordingly, Gregory supported monarchical regimes against the new democratic movements sweeping across Europe, and he declared that the divine origin of the papacy was the basis of the pope's temporal sovereignty over the papal states.[14]

Subsequent popes followed Gregory's lead. In *Quanta cura* (1864) Pius IX repeated Gregory XVI's attack on "the madness that freedom of conscience and of worship is the proper right of every human being and ought to be proclaimed by law and maintained in every rightly constituted society." In 1885 Pope Leo XIII reaffirmed the rejection of religious liberty in *Immortale Dei,* an encyclical explicitly focused upon "the Christian constitution of states." Notwithstanding what might seem the contrary implications of Leo XIII's own *Rerum Novarum* and Pope Pius XI's *Quadragesimo Anno* (1931), the Catholic church had little patience with the human rights reforms and democratic regimes of the later nineteenth and early twentieth centuries. It acquiesced in the authoritative regimes and policies that governed the European, Latin American, and African nations where Catholicism was strong. In liberal democracies, anti-Catholics had little trouble turning the church's own political philosophy against it. As recently as the 1950s, Protestant and secular elites in the United States, for example, were once again joining forces to oppose "an organization that is not only a church but a state within a state, and a state above a state."[15]

On the question of religious liberty in particular, it may be said that the Catholic church caught up with the eighteenth century only in the middle of the twentieth. In 1948 John Courtney Murray, a Jesuit professor of theology at Woodstock seminary in Maryland, presented a paper at a gathering of Catholic theologians titled "Governmental Repression of Heresy" in which he contended that it was *not* the duty of a good Catholic state to repress heresy even when it was practicable to do so. Thus the internal argument was revived, though at first it was not a fair fight. The majority of Catholic authorities, following the papal teachings, opposed Murray; his adversaries included French, German, Italian, and Spanish theologians of his own religious order. In the United States the leading expert on Catholic political philosophy had been Monsignor John A. Ryan, known as "the Right Reverend New Dealer" for his support of Franklin Delano Roosevelt's economic policies. Having studied *Mirari vos,* Ryan had concluded in 1941 that protection and promotion of Roman Catholicism is "one of the most obvious and fundamental duties of the State."[16]

Murray's opponents had a certain logic to their position, which David Hollenbach, S.J., one of Murray's intellectual heirs, summarizes as follows: "The Roman Catholic faith is the true religion. It is good for people to believe what is true. The state is obliged to promote Catholic belief, and wherever possible to establish Catholicism as the religion of the state. Advocates of religious freedom are denying one of the cardinal premises of Roman Catholicism: they are rejecting the absolute truth of Catholic Christianity."[17]

Though he was unambiguously committed to Catholic doctrine, properly interpreted, Murray argued that the received Catholic teaching on religious liberty, because it was not complete, was neither permanent nor irreformable. While consistent with the Catholic teaching since St. Augustine on the coercion of heretics, the official position ignored both apostolic and subapostolic writings on the priority of conscience, as well as St. Thomas Aquinas' teachings on the duty to follow conscience. Armed with these insights, Murray set about to challenge the dominant, semitheocratic versions of church-state theory, beginning with that propounded by St. Robert Bellarmine. The young Jesuit also retrieved the notion of "the indirect power of the Church" first elaborated by the fourteenth-century theologian Jean Quidort; and he insisted that the nineteenth-century encyclicals be read in their proper context, namely, as polemics against the anticlericalism and irreligious rationalism infecting European intellectual life at the time. The American concept of church-state separation, Murray contended, was vastly more congenial to Catholic principles.[18]

In challenging Catholic theologians to learn from the secular world and to reconsider the received doctrine in light of that learning, Murray spoke of "the growing end" of the tradition. By this he meant the contested cutting edge of the ongoing debate about what constitutes authentic Catholic teaching, the place and moment where the internal pluralism of the great tradition crystallizes into a new and profoundly transformative insight into the tradition itself. "The theological task is to trace the stages of growth of the tradition as it makes its way through history . . . to discern the elements of the tradition that are embedded in some historically conditioned synthesis that, as a synthesis, has become archaistic," Murray wrote. "The further task is to discern the 'growing end' of the tradition; it is normally indicated by the new question that is taking shape under the impact of the historical moment."[19]

Pope John XXIII's own social encyclicals, especially *Pacem in Terris* (1963), proclaimed "the universal, inviolable, inalienable rights and duties" of the human person, and presented a moral framework within which socioeconomic rights were woven together with political and civil rights. "In endorsing this spectrum of rights, including rights which are immunities and those which are empowerments, the pope took the Catholic church into the heart of the United Nations human rights debates," notes J. Bryan Hehir. "For *Pacem in Terris,* the foundation and purpose of all rights is the dignity of the human person. The scope of the rights to be endorsed as legitimate moral claims is determined by the specific needs—material and spiritual—each person has to guarantee human dignity."[20]

Murray and his allies carried the day: *Dignitatis Humanae* (*Declaration on Religious Freedom*), promulgated on December 7, 1965, ratified the postwar development of Roman Catholic doctrine on the inviolable rights of the human person and on the constitutional order of society. The council declared that human beings, directed as they are to God, "transcend by their nature the terrestrial and temporal order of things." The civil power "exceeded its limits" when it presumed to direct or impede this relationship to God. Significantly, the council declared that the right to freedom belonged to groups as well as individuals, because both human nature and religion have a social dimension.

While *Pacem in Terris* maintained a natural law framework, *Dignitatis Humanae* engaged the Enlightenment constitutional tradition of rights and liberties that affirmed the right of religious freedom. By endorsing constitutional limits on the state and by joining religious freedom with other human rights, the church embraced the full range of freedoms needed in the political order for the defense of human dignity. It did not forsake natural law, but situated it within an argument that embraced constitutional ideas previously tolerated but not accepted by the church. This development opened the way for subsequent transformations in Catholic political philosophy and social practice. By identifying innate human dignity, rather than theological orthodoxy and church membership, as the authentic source of civil rights and political self-determination, *Dignitatis Humanae* made connivance with authoritarian (albeit pro-Catholic) regimes untenable. By proclaiming that the great tradition's understanding of the freedom of the church and the limits of the state was compatible with democratic political institutions, it aligned the modern church with democratic polities and against all forms of totalitarianism.

The council's pastoral constitution, *Gaudium et Spes,* internalized the argument, so to speak, by locating the church's commitment to social justice and the promotion of human rights solidly within the ambit of its religious ministry. In this way Vatican II provided both the theological legitimation and the religious foundation for Catholic involvement in the struggle for human rights.

Precisely when the international community was considering the place of human rights and the role of transnational institutions in articulating and defending them, the Catholic Church was reshaping the perspective and structure of one of the most experienced transnational networks in history. "Substantively, Vatican II both legitimated a more activist Catholicism and provided resources for directing it," writes the legal scholar John Witte Jr. "Structurally, the council's policy of decentralization both created new transnational networks in the church and urged initiatives adapted to the local level of the church's life. The combined effect of these conciliar actions was to impel Catholicism into human rights struggles throughout the international system well into the next century."[21]

The evolution of twentieth-century Catholic social teaching, and its incorporation into the heart of the church's religious message, provided legitimation for social activism and also expanded the scope of what counted as social activism. In 1968 the Latin American bishops meeting at Medellín, Colombia, lamented the massive poverty of the continent, and focused attention on the social and political factors responsible for the oppression of the poor. Citing Vatican II, the bishops denounced what they saw as the "institutionalized violence" of Latin American society, and demanded "urgent and profoundly renovating transformations" in the social structures of their countries. The bishops urged each episcopal conference to present the church as "a catalyst in the temporal realm in an authentic attitude of service," and to support grassroots organizations for the "redress and consolidation of the rights (of the poor) and the search for justice." Catholics worldwide were urged to adopt a "preferential option for the poor" in fulfilling their political and religious responsibilities.[22]

Justice in the World, the 1971 synodal statement of Catholic bishops meeting in Rome to reflect on the legacy of the council, proclaimed a principle embraced by a generation of Catholic activists and educators: "Action on behalf of justice and participation in the transformation of the world fully appear to us as a constitutive dimension of the proclamation of the Gospel, or, in other words, of the Church's mission for the redemption of the human race and its liberation from every oppressive situation."[23]

Such proclamations initiated a postconciliar debate on the appropriate ways and means of liberating people "from every oppressive situation." By revealing and celebrating the internal pluralism of the great tradition, Vatican II had unlocked a treasury of riches—or, depending on one's perspective, a Pandora's box—filled with possibilities for innovation (via *ressourcement)* in the church's thinking on conflict and peacemaking. Catholicism is historically associated with efforts to limit violence by managing it. The just war tradition, grounded in an Augustinian theological anthropology that locates the responsibility for violence equally in the sinful nature of man, the state, and the world itself, holds that war is both the result of and remedy for sin. Coercive violence, according to this argument, may have a moral role in certain circumstances.

A second Catholic approach to the question—the legitimation of nonviolent resistance—emerged from political theory. In response to Weberian-style affirmations about the state as the entity that holds a monopoly on the legitimate use of force, Catholics argued that religion provides a different—that is, divinely ordained—authority for the use or rejection of violence. Thus the church sought either to tame the state, as in the medieval era, turning it to religious purposes and transforming it into a kind of theocracy; or it has, as in recent decades, asserted itself as a transnational alternative to and competitor with the nation-state as the ultimate arbiter of political morality.

The latter concept—the Church as moral judge of the nation-state—provided the premise for Catholic advocacy of nonviolence in concrete political settings. On this question Vatican II opened a path of practical theological reflection pursued, with different results, by Catholics across an ideological spectrum from John Paul II to Latin American liberationists. For more than a decade after the council, the church was less centralized and more socially active. Local bishops and clergy enjoyed greater autonomy in local and national affairs, and used it to bring the renewed emphasis on human rights to bear on political and cultural affairs. Roman Catholicism, once an accomplice to authoritarian regimes, thus emerged as a powerful advocate of democracy and human rights reform in Brazil, Chile, Central America, the Philippines, South Korea, and elsewhere. Under John Paul II, who became pope in 1978, Rome reasserted its prerogatives over the bishops, but the attempted recentralization did not attenuate the commitment to social justice, as demonstrated by the 1986 People's Power revolution in the Philippines, the revolution against communist rule in eastern Europe in 1989, and other nonviolent, Catholic-led revolutions against repressive governments.

Concrete applications of Catholic social principles differed significantly one from another, however. Liberation theology, inspired by the ideas of Gustavo Gutiérrez, Jon Sobrino, and other Latin American theologians, wed social scientific (and, in some cases, "Christian Marxist") analyses of political and social structures to a revisioning of the New Testament that portrayed Jesus as a radical revolutionary ("Christ the Liberator"). Organizations such as Pax Christi dedicated themselves to nonviolent activism, while missionary orders such as the Maryknoll Society became more actively involved in community development among the peoples they served. Heightened awareness of options within the church's teaching on war and peace led the bishops of the United States to include—and endorse, with qualifications—both pacifist and just war traditions in their 1983 pastoral letter on the nuclear arms race.[24]

In the decades following Vatican II, in short, the church has been alive to the possibilities presented by its complex, multinational history. In the 1980s and 1990s some national and regional Catholic leaders, responding to a central theme of the pontificate of Pope John Paul II, began to emphasize the local church's obligation to devise means of protecting and promoting human rights, especially in social settings where systemic injustices and deadly conflict feed on one another. Certain Catholic bishops, as well as lay officials of Catholic NGOs, proposed that relief and development workers adopt a more inclusive notion of community building that would require some of them to develop expertise in the growing field of intercommunal reconciliation and conflict resolution.

Catholic Relief Services' recent effort to educate its worldwide staff in the principles of Catholic social doctrine and conflict transformation nonetheless suggests how the religious tradition's social presences are evolving in the direction of nonviolent peacebuilding.

CATHOLIC RELIEF SERVICES:
NONVIOLENT PEACEBUILDING AS A CHRISTIAN PRIORITY

With relief and development programs in eighty-three countries and 1,600 professional staff residing in forty-four of them, Catholic Relief Services (CRS) is one of the world's largest international private voluntary organizations. In 1995 CRS reached more than four-teen million people in need, including two million recipients of emergency food service. Among hundreds of other initiatives, it pro-vided women in refugee camps with professional trauma counsel-ing, planned agricultural projects in sites as far removed as Bolivia and Liberia, implemented a soldier demobilization process in Sierra Leone to resettle and educate combatants and their dependents, pro-moted small-scale enterprise development (for example, village banks) in Cambodia and Vietnam, repaired refugee centers and school build-ings in Macedonia, provided relief to the victims of the civil war in the Sudan, and created a Cultural Youth Club in Sarajevo to help teenagers cope with the deprivations of the Balkans war. During the course of the year CRS workers came under fire in Bosnia, Sierra Leone, Haiti, and Cambodia; in Burundi, a staff member, Dimitri Lascaris, was assassinated.

CRS depends on funding from the United States government, which accounted for 25 percent of its budget in 1995, with the Catholic Church and individual contributors accounting for the remainder. The partnership between the U.S. government and CRS began with the organization's founding in 1943 by the U.S. Catholic bishops as an outgrowth of the church's international charitable work on behalf of refugees and workers displaced by the Second World War. In the mid-1940s CRS offices opened in Paris, Rome, and Berlin, with assistance from the local Catholic hierarchy and con-tributions of resources and personnel from Catholic religious orders such as the Daughters of Charity in France. The U.S. government, recognizing the need to rehabilitate Europe from the ground up, entered into alliances with local Catholic, Lutheran, and other churches, which became conduits for American public assistance. During its fifty-five-year history, CRS has helped coordinate U.S. private and government efforts to address international need, while lobbying the U.S. government on public policy matters affecting international relief and the status and funding of private voluntary organizations. Governmental support for CRS has been falling steadily, however, since the end of the cold war.

Inconsistency, it may be said, characterized CRS's expression of its religious identity or sponsorship. Administered by a board of bish-ops selected by the National Council of Catholic Bishops (NCCB),

CRS is staffed, its mission statement proclaims, "by men and women committed to the Catholic Church's apostolate of helping those in need." Approximately half of the international professional staff is not Roman Catholic, however, and during the 1970s and 1980s, when CRS was bolstering its reputation as a top-level professional relief agency, even the Catholics downplayed the confessional basis of the organization. "Staffers would mumble the word 'Catholic' when asked what relief agency they worked for," as one CRS official put it, "in deference to the prevailing opinion that 'religious' meant second-rate."

For much of CRS's history, the "apostolate of helping those in need" translated into traditional charitable works such as responding to victims of natural and man-made disasters and providing assistance to the poor and to victims of conflict to alleviate their immediate needs. CRS always emphasized the connection between development, peace, and justice, and it occasionally invoked Catholic social teaching, but until recently its worldwide staff members tended to think of themselves as members of a voluntary and professionalized social service agency working under religious auspices, rather than as religious or humanitarian actors educated in the social teaching of the Catholic church and trained to mediate conflict and build peaceful relations in local communities.

In this regard the experience of CRS workers in Rwanda may have been a turning point. The agency had placed field-workers there since the 1960s, yet few had developed a sophisticated understanding of the social dynamics that led to the genocide of 1994. "We were taken by surprise by the violence and its terrible intensity," one CRS official admitted. "And we asked ourselves how this could have happened, and what we needed to do to integrate ourselves into the whole life of the communities we served." The Rwanda debacle occurred just as CRS was reviewing and beginning to reconceptualize its mission.

Organizational needs and gospel imperatives converged in the U.S. Catholic bishops' response to the changed circumstances of international development agencies after the cold war. Recognizing the desirability, on financial as well as religious grounds, of developing CRS's natural Catholic constituency, the bishops acted to bring the organization more closely in line with Roman Catholicism's renewed emphasis on human rights and community building. By way of preparing CRS for new methods of serving communities divided by deadly conflict, CRS executive director Ken Hackett and his associates, under the bishops' direction, prepared a program for educating CRS professionals in the church's teaching on human rights and social justice. "By the end of 1998 the principles of Catholic Social Teaching will have transformed Catholic Relief Services," declared a 1996 internal memo touting a new five-year strategic plan. In the post–cold war world "we see that the Church will be called to play a significant role; as defender of the rights of the poor, as a voice of the oppressed, as a witness to good amidst corruption, torment, self-indulgent struggle and exploitation, as a force for love when there is hatred, as a force for moderation where there is fanaticism. We must stand in solidarity with the Church as it carries out its new evangelization." The rationale behind the new "justice lens" program went out to more than 1,600 social workers and development professionals employed as CRS field-workers:

> We cannot be truly effective until we have found practical ways to incorporate the tenets of Catholic social teaching in our management, our operations and our outlook. . . . We realize that we must work towards a fuller sense of our mission by making the promotion of social and economic justice central in our actions. We see CRS actions as part of a transformation taking place among individuals, institutions, and structures so as to assure all people a fuller human existence and dignity. . . . By placing justice as central in our operations, we expand our work of charity, open new approaches to alleviating suffering, to promoting human dignity, to building peace and respect while encouraging the participation of people in their own development. Shaping our operations more explicitly by this important element of Catholic Social Teaching, Catholic Relief Services can more explicitly affirm our Catholic identity and distinguish our work from that of other U.S. private voluntary organizations. [25]

The new orientation meant, in practice, the hiring or appointing of a small number of educators responsible for conducting two- and three-day seminars in Catholic social teaching to staff around the world. The "justice lens" seminars conveyed the church's awareness that the causes of violence in Bosnia, Rwanda, Haiti, and other conflicted areas "stem from underlying tensions found within these societies and cannot be attributed merely to a lack of social and economic development." CRS officials explained the need for the program by arguing that violent ethnic and religious conflict will become increasingly common unless right relationships are established across local religious, ethnic, economic, and political divisions. The need for professional retooling—for "conversion" to the justice lens approach on the part of Catholic as well as non-Catholic staff—was thus presented as a principled as well as a pragmatic move. "Our staff face structural injustice routinely as they carry out their mission and they naturally become involved in activities to address the situation," explained Michael Wiest, Deputy Executive Director for Overseas Operations, in 1997. "The new 'justice lens' based in Catholic social teaching will not so much alter their basic commitments as help them think more clearly in peacebuilding terms and avoid errors in their responses to social injustices. They are more vulnerable without such training."[26]

The seminars attempted to reinforce successful peacebuilding initiatives undertaken at various sites in the early 1990s. In 1994, for example, CRS staffers identified and supported local peacemakers in Zaire, Rwanda, and Burundi. In Rwanda following the genocide, all agency programming—in agricultural rehabilitation, housing, reconstruction, and support to vulnerable groups—included a component of peacebuilding and reconciliation. In Burundi CRS supported the work of the Catholic bishops who, led by Bishops Bernard Bududira and Simon Ntamwana, facilitated peace talks between parties following the April 1994 assassination of the presidents of Burundi and Rwanda.

In other settings CRS involved all ethnic groups in the rebuilding of homes and community centers that took place in the aftermath of armed conflict. In Macedonia CRS promoted interethnic dialogue between Albanian Muslims and Macedonian Orthodoxy. In El Salvador, based on its record of promoting reconciliation during twelve years of civil war and providing humanitarian assistance without partisan religious or political discrimination, CRS was asked by both former adversaries to play an active role in national reconstruction; staffers worked in the former conflict zones to reintegrate ex-combatants and to rebuild civil society through the media of agricultural production, micro-enterprise and health projects.[27]

The five-year justice strategy called first for the education of staff and partners in the principles of Catholic social teaching, followed by the building of partnership within each country between local leaders and international workers dedicated to the promotion of justice. Furthermore, the "justice lens" was to be institutionalized in management systems, domestic operations, evaluation mechanisms, and approaches to sustained learning by CRS staff and local partners—as well as by American Catholic parishioners and diocesan officials. CRS officials also anticipated the possibility of training CRS staffers in conflict resolution techniques as part of this new mission. In short, the "justice lens" plan, in the full extent of its ambition, proposed to transform CRS into a significant transnational advocate of social justice and community building.

THE PEACEBUILDING LENS

In 2002 Caritas Internationalis published *Peacebuilding: A Caritas Training Manual*. Distributed to the confederation of 154 Catholic relief and development agencies in 198 countries worldwide that comprise Caritas, the text is a companion piece to *Working for Reconciliation: A Caritas Handbook* (1999). The manual and handbook reflect the new cultural orientation of the transnational Catholic social service apostolate: the Church now strives to extend its preferential option for the poor beyond relief and charity (phase one) and beyond social and economic development (phase two), toward "reconciliation"—"a longer term process of overcoming hostility and mistrust between divided peoples . . . [and of promoting] the consolidation of constructive social relations between different groups of the population, including parties to the conflict" (*Handbook*).

The turn to culture, to the reconciliation of peoples and groups, was triggered by the experience of CRS and other Caritas member agencies working in settings of post–cold war conflicts. In the 1990s, in Rwanda, Bosnia, Sudan, Algeria, Nigeria, India, and countless other host countries, deadly violence erupted within national borders and between ethnic, religious, and cultural groups. By the time the fifteenth General Assembly of Caritas Internationalis convened in Rome in May 1995, it was already clear to the members that relief and development efforts could no longer be undertaken in isolation from cultural and communal dynamics. Nor could Catholic agencies continue to underplay their distinctive strengths as faith-based NGOs, namely, the Church's century-old tradition of teaching on social and economic justice, and, socioculturally, the natural affinity of Catholic-based transnational organizations with local Catholic churches and other religious elements within the host societies.

Accordingly, as we have seen, in the mid-1990s CRS re-viewed its mission through a "justice lens" crafted from Catholic social teaching. Annual reports and multiyear plans were evaluated, in part, according to their incorporation of projects devised to reduce or eliminate structural injustices in the host society. More recently, as indicated by the appearance of the reconciliation handbook and peacebuilding manual, Caritas Internationalis has forged a "peacebuilding lens."

And so we come to an idea in the life of the Church, which is both old and bracingly new. What could be more familiar to Christians, disciples of the Prince of Peace, than a commitment to fostering peace, forgiveness, and reconciliation? Yet what does it mean to "build peace" in a world of internecine civil, ethnic, and religious wars?

The relationship between three distinct activities—striving for social justice, resolving violent conflict, and building a sustainable peace in conflict-ridden societies—is complex. Whereas the striving for social justice has deep roots in Catholic social teaching, in the Catholic Action apostolates of the mid-twentieth century, and in the social justice and liberation theologies of the post–Vatican II church, the idea of peace*building* has emerged only recently as a complement, and perhaps a challenge, to a longer-standing modern tradition of Catholic peace*making*.

In distinguishing Catholic peacebuilding from Catholic peacemaking, it would be inaccurate, of course, to suggest that the latter has been conducted entirely apart from the grassroots activism of Catholics operating from within parishes or civic communities. But Catholic peacemaking, as I use the term here, refers to the tradition of papal and episcopal internationalism characterized by diplomatic negotiation, mediation, concordats, and settlements conducted primarily at elite governmental and ecclesial levels. Within the U.S. context, policy-relevant pastoral letters—on the economy and on the nuclear arms race, for example—are part of the peacemaking legacy, as were the U.S. Catholic Conference initiatives, in Northern Ireland, the Balkans, Sudan, and elsewhere, to stimulate local economies with direct assistance, to promote dialogue on the local and regional level, and to form partnerships to address human rights and social justice issues.

This evolving tradition of peacemaking reaches back to Pope Benedict XV's efforts to end the First World War, and it encompasses the internationalism of Pope Pius XII. Forty years ago, as we have seen, in Pope John XXIII's encyclical *Pacem in Terris,* the tradition first engaged and advanced the discourse of "human rights," thereby preparing the way for Vatican II's Declaration on Religious Freedom and for the establishment of Catholic human rights offices around the world, beginning in 1973 with the Vicariate for Solidarity, in Chile. Perhaps the high water mark of this tradition has been the emergence of the Church as a foremost advocate of universal human rights, dramatized by John Paul II's stunning elevation of human rights and religious rights above the rights and interests of the Church.

All these developments corresponded to and influenced local peacemaking efforts. But the greatest achievements—John Paul II's historic role as catalyst of Poland's Solidarity movement; the inspiration and management of nonviolent revolution in the Philippines; the mediation and implementation of peace settlements by Catholic bishops in East Timor, Chiapas, Guatemala, and elsewhere—were the result of statecraft, diplomacy, and the exercise of the Church's good offices at the pinnacle of the societal pyramid.

If the Catholic vision of peace, as articulated over the last forty years, emphasizes human rights, development, solidarity, and world order, it has placed far less emphasis on culturally resonant conflict resolution and transformation at the local and regional levels. The focus on nation-states and on foreign and defense policy reflects a line of reasoning that may need reconsideration: because nation-states make war (an assumption that is no longer universally valid), then we will be making peace if we can dissuade nation-states from this course of action. In a recent edition of its newsletter, the *Catholic Peace Fellowship* (CPF), a newly formed group of peace scholars and activists, challenges this approach to peacemaking. The bishops and their advisors at the U.S. Catholic Conference, CPF, write:

[T]ry to use their political leverage to shape the decisions of the president and the Congress [or of foreign governments]. In accord with this reasoning, the bulk of the bishops' pastoral letter on war and peace analyzed the morality of U.S. nuclear weapons policy concerning preemptive strikes, retaliatory strikes, hard-target kill strategy, and deterrence strategy. This policy-oriented approach has prevailed ever since. Most church-sponsored peacemaking efforts sought to influence the way George Bush (the father) and his staff conducted the Gulf War, or the way Bill Clinton administered the subsequent economic embargo, or the way the junior Bush and his staff conduct the present "war on terrorism." All along, the assumption has been that the things that make for peace are things decided by politicians inside the beltway. . . . But these are not the things that make for peace— not true and sustainable peace, at any rate, not the peace of Christ.[28]

The tradition now reaches a new point in its development. The nature of warfare has changed; conflicts are "identity conflicts" erupting within national borders; the enemy may be one's literal neighbor. For peacebuilders in this era, the local is the center of gravity; efforts for peace begin "from the ground up" and selectively engage state and international centers of economic, political, and military power, where Catholic peacemaking heretofore has concentrated energies and intellects. *Working for Reconciliation* makes explicit the shift in orientation: "As we look back on the history of peacemaking and peace processes we see that they have traditionally centered on diplomacy, mediation, the cessation of hostilities and the achievement of peace agreements. These things we are all familiar with. Once a peace agreement is signed the diplomats and mediators go home and parties to the conflict get on with life under the terms of the peace agreement. *This is not sufficient any more.*"[29]

What must be developed, the handbook continues, are cohorts of indigenous peacebuilders—agents for nonviolent change who, as members of the society experiencing strife, have a vested and long-term interest in applying their irreplaceable "local knowledge" to the task of reconciliation. Such local and regional conciliators have become essential actors "because peace settlements do not bring about the required change of heart, which is the crux of peace, particularly in complex internal conflicts."[30]

Peacebuilding thus precedes and follows upon peacemaking, which is a specific moment in the larger process. The conflict mediators and diplomats, if they are successful, bring a halt to the killing and abuse, at least temporarily, through negotiated settlements and political solutions. By defusing immediate tensions, they make peace possible. Peacebuilders, however, make peace *real*—they work over months, years, and decades, that is, to sustain the peace, to transform nonviolent conflict resolution and, where possible, reconciliation, into a way of life. "The principle of indigenous empowerment suggests that conflict transformation must actively envision, include, respect and promote the human and cultural resources from within a given setting," writes peacebuilding scholar-practitioner John Paul Lederach. "This involves a new set of lenses through which we see the setting and the people not as the problem and the outsider as the answer. Rather, we understand the long-term goal of transformation as validating and building on people and resources within the setting."[31]

LEARNING FROM THE PEACE(BUILDING) CHURCHES

The twentieth century witnessed a remarkable convergence of historical trajectories, one unfolding within the Roman Catholic Church and the other within the peace churches (churches of the broad Anabaptist tradition—e.g., the Mennonites, Church of the Brethren, the Quakers—which originated in the radical wing of the Reformation).

From Dorothy Day to *The Challenge of Peace* to *The Harvest of Justice Is Sown in Peace* (1993), U.S. Catholics followed a path that led them to acknowledge and eventually to endorse the pacifist option found within the New Testament and the early church, and to develop a theology of nonviolent resistance to complement traditional just war theory. Meanwhile, during and after the world wars the peace churches, those who had earned the name from their longstanding and exclusive commitment to nonviolence, reexamined their attitudes toward the sinful, blood-soaked world and gradually abandoned a strict separatist stance. The Mennonites, for example, after devoting energies to humanitarian assistance and service to peoples in need, turned in the 1970s and 1980s to the work of international conciliation and, eventually, to peacebuilding. Through "bridge-builders" such as the distinguished Mennonite theologian John

Howard Yoder, who taught for many years at Notre Dame, Mennonites and Catholics began to share ideas and methods.[32]

Lederach, one of the lead authors of the new Caritas manual, is a Mennonite who gained prominence as a creative and insightful conceptualizer of the peacebuilding trajectory and practice. In recent years, as Catholics have gotten their own peacebuilding house in order, Lederach has gravitated to Catholic circles in response to what he calls "admiration of Catholic verticality." By this he means that the Catholic Church's pervasive presence in dozens of nations and its hierarchical, pyramidal structure ensures that the Christian (or other faith-based) practitioner of nonviolent conflict transformation and peacebuilding will find potential Catholic allies across the globe, in one conflict zone after another, embedded (to use the word of the day) at each level of society. Hence, the "verticality": Cardinals, archbishops, and wealthy or politically powerful or otherwise influential lay Catholics are found among the elites of society; Catholic intellectuals and cultural leaders, bishops, influential priests and religious, and Catholic NGOs operate within civil society, in crucial mid-level leadership positions; and priests, religious and laity ministering to and teaching in the towns, villages, and parishes constitute important elements of the grass roots. These potential partners are natural allies because they are committed in principle both to social justice and to peacemaking.

The qualifying words "potential" and "in principle" suggest where to find the "growing end of the argument." Lederach and other non-Catholics are learning, as they train and collaborate with Catholics in peacebuilding, that the ubiquitous Catholic presence at various levels of some societies does not automatically translate into a coherent or compatible company of peace and justice allies. We Catholics could have told them: there is one Body, but there are many members, and they do not subscribe to the same ideology or theology (or ecclesiology) of peace and justice. And even where one finds common purpose and virtual political-theological harmony, if not perfect consensus, among Catholics occupying different social positions within "the vertical Church," another problem arises: one hand often does not know what the other is doing.

And yet the overall picture is encouraging, the potential astounding. One need only look to the dizzying array of recent and current

Caritas and other Catholic relief, development, and justice programs and projects to find an antidote to the "American Catholic blues"—the cloud of depression that has descended upon the Church in the United States as a result of years of lamenting institutional downsizing, the diminishing numbers of practicing and religiously literate Catholics, and, now, the further enfeeblement attendant upon the sexual abuse crisis. The *Handbook* alone lists more than 120 organizations working around the world in conflict resolution (not all of them Catholic, but most are partners or potential partners) and profiles twenty-four "examples of good practice in reconciliation" conducted by Catholics and their nongovernmental partners in the field. Such exemplary practices include trauma healing in Croatia; human rights advocacy in Guatemala; conflict prevention and mitigation in Ahmedabad, India; Muslim-Christian peacebuilding workshops in Mindanao, Philippines; education for peace in Egypt; and conflict resolution training in Sierra Leone. The Church universal, in short, is thriving in its mission to civil society.

This range of activity comes after, and partly in response to, the end of the cold war, the proliferation of transnational social movements and nongovernmental organizations, the outbreak or renewal of ethnic and religious conflicts. It is also emerging as a result of the success of Catholic social teaching in being absorbed into the bloodstream of Catholic charities, relief services, lay movements such as the Community of Sant'Egidio—and even into the consciousness and practices of the historic peace churches: the influence runs in both directions.

Catholic peacebuilders, furthermore, are now present at every stage of the conflict transformation cycle: they work in peace education and conflict prevention, in mediation and conflict resolution, in postsettlement social reconstruction, and in the academies and courts where human rights, including religious freedom, are given theoretical depth and cross-cultural grounding. The training grounds for Catholics seeking entry into this emerging world of peacebuilding increasingly include the local parish and inner city ministries of reconciliation and conflict resolution.

One also finds encouragement in lay movements such the Community of Sant'Egidio, whose work of disciplined friendship and service to the poor and marginalized, coupled with the professional

background and political and religious access of the members, has
made the community an international leader in conflict mediation
and transformation. Catholics are collaborating in new and productive ways with government and nongovernmental organizations.
The Maryknoll Research Center and the United States Institute of
Peace work together to advance Christian-Muslim understanding
and dialogue on the grass roots and middle levels of society, through
programs and research projects that examine the respective traditions, teachings, and practices in the areas of human rights, tolerance, and mission. The would-be Catholic peacebuilder might also
find an institutional partner in the World Conference on Religion and Peace, which brings local religious and cultural leaders
together in chapters dedicated to joint initiatives promoting the
building up of interethnic, interreligious cultures of nonviolence
through such measures as the establishment of joint library, publications, and interreligious councils in the war-torn regions of Bosnia
and Sierra Leone.[33]

Ideally, this new dimension of Catholic peacemaking engages
grass-roots *and* middle-range leaders *and* elites in a coherent, coor-
dinated strategy; it draws upon the Catholic Church's great strength
as a hierarchical, transnational, multicultural institution and community; and it does all this with a heightened level of intentionality and
self-awareness and a striving for coherence that may be possible only
in the kind of globalized, high-tech, communications-immersed and
cyberspace-driven world we now inhabit.

Perhaps it is primarily in this last respect—in the level of intentionality—that we can identify "peacebuilding" as something new
in Catholic peacemaking. But the heightened awareness and intentionality is leading us to more inclusive and dynamic patterns of
cross-religious and religious-secular collaboration than those we have
enjoyed, or failed to enjoy, in the past.

FROM WEAK TO STRONG PEACEBUILDING

Heightened awareness also prompts us to recognize and name
underdeveloped dimensions of Catholic peacebuilding as it is emerging within Catholic institutions and groups, and beyond Catholic

institutions and groups. Three currently weak dimensions deserve comment in this context.

First, a lack of communication and sharing of resources across levels of Catholic peacebuilding and justice building prevents the Church from being more effective in this important apostolic work. The list of ideas and peacebuilding initiatives *is* dizzying. While there is great wisdom in letting a thousand flowers bloom, there is also strength and success in communication and coordination of efforts. Better communication up and down and across the pyramid would serve to consolidate and thus conserve resources and energies, and it would enhance the opportunities for collaboration and sharing of resources, including field experiences and the insights and stories cultivated from them.

Catholic verticality, Lederach laments, is largely an untapped resource. Too frequently the efforts of the hierarchy and their colleagues are uninformed by what is happening, or could be happening, at the grass roots. Even more disabling is the failure to develop and utilize the crucial "middle management"—the Catholic administrators, intellectuals, public servants, NGOs, and so on—who could serve as the organic link between elite peacemakers and the local peacebuilders. The levels of communication and coordination vary, Lederach acknowledges, but every Catholic setting he has visited, from Colombia to the Philippines, needs help in this area. Unless Catholics can "actualize verticality," as he puts it, the Church cannot begin to realize its vast potential to build peaceful societies over the long term.[34]

A second concern regarding the new peacebuilding trajectory is the temptation to conceive the work of peace and justice as a technical, process-bound, social scientific enterprise (by which planners with organizational blueprints in hand conspire to "actualize verticality"). Some Catholics worry about a tendency toward overmanagement and the replication, ironically, of secular-bureaucratic, instrumentalist models.

But that is not what Catholic peacebuilders and their ecumenical partners envision or desire. To the contrary, they argue that effective methods of peace education, conflict management, and reconciliation within divided communities, which would be stimulated by greater levels of communication and coordination, serve authentic human development. Planning, coordination, and analysis based on culturally nuanced and religiously sophisticated diagnosis of a conflict setting is a work of the people, not of bureaucracies. It does not replace but complements and gives concrete social expression to the proclamation of the gospel and the works of mercy. Those who worry about mega-management, after reflecting for a moment on the decentralized, local nature of the Church, will be reassured of the persistence of spontaneity and unfettered creativity at the local and regional levels.

Nor should we take a "let the Spirit blow where it will" attitude when considering the need for professionally trained, vocationally inspired peacebuilders. At the higher levels of Catholic peacemaking, the Church has relied on full-time professionals, while allowing a kind of serendipity to reign at lower levels, where NGOs, student volunteers, and others gather. Lederach muses about a day when a "religious order of conciliators" might emerge—peacebuilding pioneers who will develop the praxis of a just peace "from the ground up," wherever the Catholic Church is present in a humanitarian capacity.

Already some Catholics have voiced a third concern about the new orientation of Catholic peace and justice, namely, that it is insufficiently Catholic. Objections of this kind, to the extent that they are driven reflexively by the tired identity politics of the U.S. Catholic culture wars, can be summarily dismissed. The knee-jerk rejection of substantive collaboration with non-Catholics, including other Christians, contravenes the letter as well as the spirit of Vatican II, as well as the teaching of Pope John Paul II.

If Catholics do not focus attention upon developing the theological and ecclesiological foundations of Catholic peacebuilding, however, such concerns could become legitimate. Drew Christiansen, S.J., who has contributed significantly to top-down Catholic peacemaking in his work for the USCC, has joined Lederach in calling for the articulation of a constructive Theology of Just Peace. The resources for such a theology include the distinctively Christian scriptural, ethical, and theological teachings about peace. These principles and testimony regarding the priority of grace should prevent Catholics and other Christians from confusing peace, a gift of God and a participation in Christ's reign, with a secular peace, understood as the achievable end of a technical, rationalized, and instrumental process. Such a theology must also draw, however, upon the moral imagination of Christian peacebuilders already on the ground. They are our guides in constructing a positive vision of what peace might be, and what concrete social and psychological conditions provide for a sustainable just peace in their homeland.

CONCLUSION

Any comprehensive, all-encompassing model for nonviolent peacebuilding will always be developed on the basis of sustained cross-cultural dialogue and storytelling. And because Vatican II taught Catholics to take history seriously and to discern and adapt to historical change, any such model will necessarily be provisional. And yet, the developments within Roman Catholicism during the human rights era enabled the church to sharpen its understanding of the distinction between society and the state, and to align itself more closely with the diverse communities, forms of association, and voluntary agencies of the former. Only in this way could nonviolent peacebuilding become a concrete possibility, not only for Catholics, but for the ecumenical school of nonviolence profiled in the first section of this essay. Developing peacebuilding programs and praxis within the range of Christian communities is now a work in progress.

NOTES

1. John Howard Yoder, *The Politics of Jesus* (Notre Dame, Ind.: University of Notre Dame Press, 1972), 97.

2. Jürgen Moltmann, *The Spirit of Life: A Universal Affirmation,* translated by Margaret Kohl (Minneapolis: Fortress, 1992), 130.

3. For a classic statement, see John A. Ryan and Francis J. Boland, *Catholic Principles of Politics* (New York: Macmillan, 1948).

4. Yoder, *The Politics of Jesus,* 90.

5. Ibid.

6. Miroslav Volf, *Exclusion and Embrace: A Theological Exploration of Identity, Otherness, and Reconciliation* (Nashville: Abingdon Press, 1996).

7. Moltmann, *The Spirit of Life,* 137.

8. Donald W. Shriver Jr., *An Ethic for Enemies: Forgiveness in Politics* (New York: Oxford University Press, 1995).

9. Volf, *Exclusion and Embrace,* 26.

10. As Jonathan Schell argues in his latest book, *The Unconquerable World: Power, Nonviolence, and the Will of the People* (New York: Metropolitan Books, 2003).

11. Judith M. Brown, *Gandhi, Prisoner of Hope* (New Haven: Yale University Press, 1989).

12. Chris Hedges, "Response: Religion as an Antidote to Peacemaking," Harvard Center for the Study of the World's Religions, unpublished remarks, 1999.

13. These tenets came to include: 1) *the common good,* the notion that Catholics ought to pursue policies and programs that best serve the interests of the public at large rather than a particular subgroup within society (including Roman Catholics); 2) *solidarity,* the affirmation that all people—and all religions—at every level of society should participate together in building a just society; 3) *subsidiarity,* the dictum that greater and higher associations or governing bodies ought not to do what lesser and lower (more local) associations can do themselves (a sort of Catholic federalism); 4) *a preferential option for the poor,* a principle with concrete implications for politicians, governments, development economists, corporate executives, and policymakers; 5) *the priority and inviolablilty of human rights,* especially the cornerstone right to life, but also political and economic rights, including the right to own private property, the right to work for a just wage, and (some progressives would argue) the right to adequate medical care; and 6) *a preferential option for the family* as the basic social unit.

14. Richard P. McBrien, *Lives of the Popes: The Pontiffs from St. Peter to John Paul II* (New York: Harper Collins, 1997), 338; Josef L. Althholz, *The Churches in the Nineteenth Century* (New York: Bobbs-Merrill, 1967), 55–90.

15. Paul Blanshard, *American Freedom and Catholic Power* (Boston: Beacon Press, 1949), 4.

16. John A. Ryan and Francis J. Boland, *Catholic Principles of Politics* (New York: Macmillan, 1948), 319; John T. Noonan Jr., *The Lustre of Our Country: The American Experience of Religious Freedom* (Berkeley, Calif.: University of California Press, 1998), 26–27.

17. David Hollenbach, S.J., "The Growing End of an Argument," *America* 30 (November 30, 1985): 364.

18. Noonan, *The Lustre of Our Country,* 28; see also J. Leon Hooper, S.J., "The Theological Sources of John Courtney Murray's Ethics," in J. Leon Hooper, S.J., and Todd David Whitmore, eds., *John Courtney Murray and the Growth of Tradition* (Kansas City: Sheed and Ward, 1997), 106–25.

19. John Courtney Murray, S.J., "The Problem of Religious Freedom," *Theological Studies* 25 (1964): 569.

20. J. Bryan Hehir, "Religious Activism for Human Rights: A Christian Case Study," in John Witte Jr. and Johan D. van der Vyver, *Religious Human Rights in Global Perspective: Religious Perspectives* (The Hague, Netherlands: Martinus Nijhoff, 1996), 103. At the time *Pacem in Terris* was written, debate in the United Nations centered on the question of which rights were to be given primacy, and whether all the claims found in U.N. texts were truly rights. Set in the broader ideological struggle of the Cold War, this debate saw the socialist system endorsing socioeconomic rights, with Western democracies giving priority to civil and political rights. *Pacem in Terris* provided an authoritative framework for an understanding of human rights within the church and influenced the public debate as well, Hehir notes.

21. John Witte Jr., "Introduction," 12.

22. "Medellín Documents: Poverty of the Church," in Gremillion, *The Gospel of Peace and Justice,* 471–76.

23. "Justice in the World," in ibid., 514.

24. U.S. Catholic Bishops, *The Challenge of Peace: God's Promise and Our Response* (Washington, D.C.: United States Catholic Conference, 1983). On Pax Christ, see John A. Coleman and Thomas Leininger, "Discipleship as Non-Violence, Citizenship as Vigilance," in John A. Coleman, ed., *Religion, Discipleship, and Citizenship* (forthcoming). While the social justice path is usually associated with nonviolent activism, Catholic liberationists in Latin America and other parts of the developing world have interpreted Catholic arguments in favor of universal human rights and economic justice as sufficient warrant for taking up arms in wars of liberation against oppressive regimes—a position the Vatican has repeatedly condemned as an inappropriate application of the preferential option for the poor.

25. "CRS Strategic Plan Summary, 1996–2001," private circulation, Catholic Relief Services, Baltimore.

26. Personal interview, March 22, 1997.

27. Internal memo (no date), Archives Library Research Center, Catholic Relief Services, Baltimore, Md.

28. Editorial, *The Sign of Peace: Journal of the Catholic Peace Fellowship* 1, no. 1: 3.

29. *Working for Reconciliation: A Caritas Handbook* (Vatican City: Caritas Internationalis, 1999), 3.

30. Ibid., 6.

31. Quoted in *Working for Reconciliation: A Caritas Handbook* (Vatican City: Caritas Internationalis, 1992), 6.

32. This story of recent Mennonite-Catholic collaboration is presented in Drew Christiansen's article "An Exchange of Gifts," *America,* March 3, 2003.

33. On these developments, see R. Scott Appleby, *The Ambivalence of the Sacred: Religion, Conflict, and Reconciliation* (Lanham, Md.: Rowman & Littlefield, 2000), chapter 4.

34. See, inter alia, John Paul Lederach, *The Journey Toward Reconciliation* (Scottsdale, Penn.: Herald Press, 1999).

ABOUT THE CONTRIBUTORS

R. Scott Appleby, Ph.D.
R. Scott Appleby, professor of history at the University of Notre
Dame, is the John M. Regan Jr. Director of the University's Joan
B. Kroc Institute for International Peace Studies. A historian of reli-
gion who earned a Ph.D. from the University of Chicago (1985),
Appleby is author of *The Ambivalence of the Sacred: Religion, Violence,
and Reconciliation* (Rowman & Littlefield, 2000) and coauthor, with
Gabriel Almond and Emmanuel Sivan, of *Strong Religion: The Rise of
Fundamentalisms Around the World* (2003). With Martin E. Marty, he
directed the Fundamentalist Project and edited the five volumes on
global fundamentalism published by the University of Chicago Press
from 1991 to 1995. Appleby is also the author of *Church and Age
Unite! The Modernist Impulse in American Catholicism* (1992), coeditor
of *Being Right: Conservative Catholics in America* (1995), and coauthor
of *Transforming Parish Ministry: The Changing Roles of Clergy, Laity, and
Women Religious* (1989). He is currently directing a Cushwa Center
research project on American Catholicism in the twentieth century.

His Eminence Dr. Mustafa Ceric
Dr. Mustafa Ceric is the *Reis-ul-Ulema,* president of the Council
of *Ulema,* Grand Mufti of Bosnia-Herzegovina. He graduated from
the Medressa in Sarajevo and received a scholarship to Al Azhar University in Cairo. Subsequently, he returned to his native Bosnia, where
he became an Imam. In 1981, he accepted the position of Imam at
the Islamic Cultural Center and settled in the United States for several years. He learned English and earned a Ph.D. at the University
of Chicago in Islamic Theology. When he finished his studies, he
returned to his homeland, left the ICC, and became a practicing
Imam in a learning center in Zagreb in 1987. He authored *Roots
of Synthetic Theology in Islam: A Choice between War and Peace,* among
other publications in Bosnian.

Rabbi Reuven Firestone, Ph.D.

Reuven Firestone was educated at Antioch College; the Hebrew University in Jerusalem; Hebrew Union College, where he received his M.A. in Hebrew literature in 1980 and rabbinic ordination in 1982; and New York University, where he received his Ph.D. in Arabic and Islamic studies in 1988. From 1987 to 1992, he taught Hebrew literature and directed the Hebrew and Arabic language programs at Boston University. Since 1993, he has served as associate and then full professor of medieval Judaism and Islam at Hebrew Union College–Jewish Institute of Religion, Los Angeles, where he directs the Edgar F. Magnin School for Graduate Studies. In 2000, Rabbi Firestone was awarded a fellowship for independent research from the National Endowment for the Humanities for his research on holy war in Judaism, and was chosen to be a fellow of the Institute for Advanced Jewish Studies at the University of Pennsylvania in 2002. He has authored three books and dozens of articles on Islam, Judaism, and Jewish-Muslim relations.

Rabbi Irving Greenberg, Ph.D.

Rabbi Irving Greenberg is the president of Jewish Life Network (JLN), a Judy and Michael Steinhardt Foundation. JLN's mission is to create new institutions and initiatives to enrich the inner life (religious, cultural, institutional) of American Jewry. Rabbi Greenberg served as chairman of the United States Holocaust Memorial Council from 2000 to 2002. He has written extensively on the theory and practice of pluralism, on the theology of Jewish-Christian relations, and on the ethics of Jewish power. An ordained Orthodox rabbi, a Harvard Ph.D., and a scholar, Rabbi Greenberg has published numerous articles and monographs on Jewish thought and religion, including *The Jewish Way: Living the Holidays* (1988), a philosophy of Judaism based on an analysis of the Sabbath and holidays, and *Living in the Image of God: Jewish Teachings to Perfect the World* (1998).

Fr. James L. Heft, S.M., Ph.D.

Fr. James L. Heft, S.M. (Marianist), is the founding director and president of the Institute for Advanced Catholic Studies at the University of Southern California. He is currently on leave from the

University of Dayton, where he is University Professor of Faith and Culture, and chancellor. He is the author of *John XXII (1316–1334) and Papal Teaching Authority* (1986), and editor of *Faith and the Intellectual Life* (1996), and *A Catholic Modernity? The Marianist Award Lecture of Charles Taylor* (1999). He is currently working on a book on Catholic higher education. His article "Mary of Nazareth, Feminism and the Tradition," coauthored by Dr. Una Cadegan, won the 1990 Catholic Press Association award for best scholarly article. He has published more than 150 articles, encyclopedia entries, book chapters, and book reviews, and serves on the editorial board of two scholarly journals.

Mohamed Fathi Osman, Ph.D.
Professor Osman is director of the Institute for the Study of the Role of Islam in the Contemporary World and scholar in residence at the Omar Ibn Al-Khattab Foundation. He received a B.A. in history from Cairo University, a J.D. from Alexandria University, an M.A. in Islamic Relations from Cairo University, and a Ph.D. in Islamic History from Princeton University. He has held academic positions in Saudi Arabia, Malaysia, Egypt, the United States, and Algeria. He has published numerous works in both Arabic and English throughout his more than forty-year career. In 2000, Prof. Osman was recognized by the American Muslim Council for his "outstanding intellectual contribution" to Islam and received the Excellence Award.

Leonard Swidler, Ph.D.
Leonard Swidler, professor of Catholic Thought and Interreligious Dialogue at Temple University, holds degrees in history, philosophy, and theology from Marquette University (M.A.), University of Wisconsin (Ph.D.), and Tübingen University in Germany (S.T.L.). He has been a visiting professor at universities in Austria, Germany, China, Malaysia, and Japan, and has lectured at Fudan University, Shanghai; National Chen Chi University, Taiwan; Bosnian Academy of Science and Arts, Sarajevo; Austrian Academy of Sciences, Vienna; the second Vienna Culture Congress; the fourth Conference on Religious Liberty, Sao Paulo, Brazil; the 2000 Jewish-Christian-Muslim Scholars Dialogue in Jakarta, Indonesia; at Dongguk Buddhist University, Seoul, Korea; and in Hiroshima, Japan. He is editor of the

Journal of Ecumenical Studies, and since 1964, he has published more than 175 articles and 60 books, including *After the Absolute* (1990); *For All Life: Toward a Universal Declaration of a Global Ethic. An Interreligious Dialogue* (1998); *Theoria to Praxis. How Jews, Christians, Muslims Can Together Move from Theory to Practice* (1999); and *The Study of Religion in the Age of Global Dialogue* (2000).

Charles Taylor, Ph.D.

Charles Taylor is professor emeritus of philosophy at McGill University in Montreal, Canada. He is Board of Trustees Professor of Law and Philosophy at Northwestern University and a member of the academic advisory council of the Institute for Advanced Catholic Studies. Professor Taylor has also taught at Yale, New York University, Hebrew University, Stanford, Oxford, and Princeton. Born in Montreal, Canada, Prof. Taylor received his B.A. from McGill University and his M.A. and Ph.D. from Oxford University. He has authored more than a dozen books, including *Sources of the Self* (1989), *The Ethics of Authenticity* (1992), and *Varieties of Religion Today* (2002). He is currently preparing a publication on modern secular civilization.

INDEX